An Unlikely Dilemma

CHURCH OF SWEDEN
Research Series

Göran Gunner, editor
Vulnerability, Churches, and HIV (2009)

Kajsa Ahlstrand and Göran Gunner, editors
Non-Muslims in Muslim Majority Societies (2009)

Jonas Ideström, editor
For the Sake of the World (2010)

Göran Gunner and Kjell-Åke Nordquist
An Unlikely Dilemma (2011)

An Unlikely Dilemma

Constructing a Partnership
between Human Rights and Peace-Building

GÖRAN GUNNER *and* KJELL-ÅKE NORDQUIST

☛PICKWICK *Publications* · Eugene, Oregon

AN UNLIKELY DILEMMA
Constructing a Partnership between Human Rights and Peace-Building

Church of Sweden Research Series 4

Church of Sweden Research Unit in cooperation with Diakonia, Sweden, and the Research Program on Human Rights and Peace-Building, Stockholm School of Theology, Sweden.

Pickwick Publications
An Imprint of Wipf and Stock Publishers
199 W. 8th Ave., Suite 3
Eugene, OR 97401

www.wipfandstock.com

ISBN 13: 978-1-61097-272-7

Cataloging-in-Publication data:

An unlikely dilemma : constructing a partnership between human rights and peace-building / Göran Gunner and Kjell-Åke Nordquist.

xii + 180 p. ; 23 cm. Including bibliographical references.

Church of Sweden Research Series 4

ISBN 13: 978-1-61097-272-7

1. Human rights. 2. Peace-building. I. Title. II. Series.

JZ5538 U55 2011

Manufactured in the U.S.A.

Contents

About the Authors

Göran Gunner
Associate Professor in Mission Studies, Uppsala University, and Researcher at Church of Sweden Research Unit, Uppsala. Dr Gunner is also Senior Lecturer at Stockholm School of Theology, Stockholm, Sweden.

Kjell-Åke Nordquist
Associate Professor in Peace and Conflict Research, Uppsala University, and Visiting Professor and Head of Research Program on Human Rights and Peace-Building, Stockholm School of Theology, Stockholm, Sweden.

Foreword

THIS STUDY HAS ITS roots in an ongoing dialogue between researchers at Stockholm School of Theology and Church of Sweden Research Unit, as well as with a number of non-governmental organizations, national and international, in the fields of human rights, peace, and development.

It is part of the outcome from the Research Program on Human Rights and Peace-Building at Stockholm School of Theology, supported by Swedish Diakonia, Church of Sweden Research Unit, as well as other donors.

Part of the preparation for this study has been a series of activities, in Sweden and internationally, that were organized with the purpose of casting light on the relationship between the human rights and peace-building agendas. Besides invited studies, guest scholars, seminars, study visits, also dialogues between practitioners and academics have been held on different continents of the world.

Co-writing a book-length text is in itself an undertaking that requires—besides a good sense of humor—time and effort and mutual understanding. The theme of this study adds an extra dimension to this necessary convergence of ideas. We invite the reader to share the labor and joy from this work.

Stockholm, January 2011
Göran Gunner
Kjell-Åke Nordquist

Figures and Tables

1

An Unlikely Dilemma

*—The transition to democracy in Chile was shameful.
There were too many human rights concessions to the military.*

—So the concessions were basically unnecessary?

*—No, they were necessary and shameful—at the same time.
It had not been possible without them!*

(From a discussion twenty years after democracy
was introduced in Chile after military rule.)

HUMAN RIGHTS AND PEACE-BUILDING represent principles and
working methods that go well together hand-in-hand—at least,
this is what we have reason to believe. However, interfaces between the
two traditions nevertheless are exposed to friction in various situations,
be they normative, policy-related or operational. Organizational structures add to this friction. In many countries civil society is organized in
a way that indicates a separation between what we throughout this study
will label the Human Rights and Peace-Building agendas, respectively.
The same situation is reflected as well in the internal organization of
agencies and ministries in many countries. This is true, as we shall see,
even for the United Nations.

Nevertheless, organizations, individual practitioners and scholars—
recognizing the risk for division—try to bring the perspectives closer
together and even integrate them both in theory and action.[1] Still, in
some situations the Human Rights and Peace-Building agendas lead to

1. An important contribution in this respect is Mertus and Helsing, *Human Rights
and Conflict*.

1

different approaches, different actions, and sometimes-contradictory ways of approaching the very same, concrete situation. Cooperation and mutually reinforcing strategies under such circumstances are a long way off. Instead a narrow struggle between agendas and their practical implications is far more likely.

In times of conflict and war, human rights are challenged more than ever and are thus more necessary to defend than ever. When "war" turns into "post-war"—by force or by free will of the parties—human rights are by that very process strengthened in certain ways: less lives are taken, humanitarian and other forms of support can reach those that are in need, and life can gradually return to more civilized routines.

The problem is, however, that reaching this point, where "war" makes a turn into "post-war," is not made by following a clear-cut and straightforward road map. And in the first place: it requires good reasons for the parties to actually embark on such a journey. If these reasons are not there, fighting for one or all of the parties is what is preferred, or it is simply what they feel they have to do. And that means—again—violations of human rights and sometimes International Humanitarian Law (IHL), widespread destruction, and continued division between individuals and societies.

Given that the goal of both peace-building and human rights is a lasting peace with justice and development—the formula can be phrased in different ways—friction between the two agendas cannot be regarded as something that is impossible to deal with. Instead the question has to be about what can be done to deal with such a situation.

This dilemma, created by the so-called peace vs. justice debate among the international community of states, international organizations, and NGOs, has been felt increasingly in recent decades. There has been a substantial development of issues and responsibilities within both the Human Rights and Peace-Building agendas since the end of the Cold War. In comparison to previous decades, the 1990s and also the first decade of the new millennium have seen some significant peace processes, such as in Central America, Southern and West Africa, and in Southeast Asia. For the Human Rights agenda, the establishment of the International Criminal Court indicates an institutionalization of a human rights instrument of a magnitude never seen before. Vast collections of experiences and insights have been gathered in both the Peace-Building and the Human Rights agendas over the years. They represent sources of trust and inspiration for millions in a world without peace and justice.

Most armed conflicts today are internal. This means in practice that the population sooner or later becomes involved and affected. In some cases guerilla groups have support among the local population against the country's rulers, in other cases populations are held hostage by one or both sides. In all cases, civilians are suffering. "Winning" in a traditional sense is in most cases not a realistic prospect, neither militarily nor politically in such conflicts. Fighting as part of the conflict is not always regular. Therefore, whenever a conflict threatens to be serious and lasting, the local and the international community has an interest to stop fighting through peaceful means rather than strengthening one of the parties' military capacity. This creates pressing issues requiring moral and political judgments. The key problem has two sides: how to get those (often leaders) whose human rights record needs to be scrutinized to accept this scrutiny, since they have the opportunity to escape this until an agreement is signed? Why—they think—give up personal security, and—since few conflicts are morally black and white—why do it when individuals "on the other side" seem to escape the same scrutiny? The other side of the problem presents itself to the democratic community, foreign states and their international organizations. They will have to ask if one should negotiate at all with perpetrators of human rights violations—and if so, under what conditions?

In cases of gradual transition from military rule to a democratic system, to take a similar case, many military governments with records of severe human rights violations have decided to grant themselves amnesty to secure their future after handing over power to an elected and democratic government. In some cases, even after decades, these democratic states have come to a point where it has been possible to revise these amnesty laws. In other cases this has not (yet) been the case. In many cases, the perpetrators—who should have been brought to justice—could escape this fate due to the length of these processes. This balancing act, between ongoing conflict and compromising with human rights because there is not enough strength to do otherwise, is an unwanted dilemma that must necessarily be dealt with. The dilemma is part of the general problem addressed in this study.

Another dilemma is how resources should be spent once the violence ends and peace—if only as a commitment, very shaky, and limited—is in place to allow for new initiatives, new institutions, and new perspectives. What priority has justice for survivors and generally targeted groups? What priority has civil and political rights, as well as social, economic, and cultural rights? To what extent are the rights of women and children safeguarded? While human rights relate to a broad development agenda, and while all situations lack resources, particularly after armed conflict, what should be the priorities and what—if any—can be left to a coming future?

The earlier in an armed conflict that negotiations begin the stronger the parties are and, therefore, the less likely they are to accept a negotiated outcome. The incentive for a party to stop fighting has to be bigger than the incentive to continue. Is the achievement of a fragile peace worth its price if it means justice will have to wait and perhaps facing the risk that it will never be achieved? Is continued fighting to be preferred over compromising fundamental rights to justice and compensation for victims?

The conflict in the Balkans (i.e., the breakup of Yugoslavia) showed that the level of economic development of a country is not a protection against certain forms of human rights violations or crimes against humanity—by governments or by other actors. For a long period countries like the Democratic Republic of Congo, Somalia, Sudan, Afghanistan, and Colombia have illustrated how similar events appear, with a steady repetition in media. In all of these countries the issue has been brought to the table: if we manage to get a cease-fire and eventually some peace and stability, shall we allow this to be threatened by bringing former perpetrators of serious human rights violations to court even if stability is not secured in the society? Or rather: is it possible to justify that such legal processes are worth waiting until stability is achieved—and if so, how do we know when *it is* achieved?

These situations have been dealt with in various ways in a variety of countries. In Chile and Argentina, for instance, it took some fifteen years to initiate a gradual change of legislation that made it possible to bring military perpetrators to justice through the courts of their current democratic governments. In Liberia, only a few years ago, the international community (mainly the African Union and the UN) brought democratic elections and a new government to the country after a negotiated defeat of the rebels and their leader, Charles Taylor. By forcing him to leave Liberia it was later possible to transfer him to the International Criminal Court in The Hague, Netherlands, and in this way he was brought to justice.

It is probably fair to say that the mere formulation of the question as being dichotomous, as is done above, is creating a way of thinking that goes against the purpose of this study. Still, this is a point of departure that illustrates a dilemma and a theme for investigation that is not (only) an academic, but a real-life issue to be dealt with. While the basis for a human rights perspective is founded in a particular view of the human being and the concept of dignity, its practical formulation, or "operationalization," has for long been in the form of international declarations, conventions, and agreements, as well as in International Humanitarian Law. Put in a single sentence, a Human Rights agenda is based on the principle that "all human beings are born free and equal in dignity and rights."[2] A Peace-Building agenda lacks this stage of being internationally agreed or ratified in documents. In line with the UN Charter, peace-building has as its guiding principles cooperation, mutual respect, justice, and fairness. If a single fundamental principle should be formulated for the peace-building perspective it is probably a *trust-based principle*. Without a certain degree of trust, even if very low, any political order would be impossible.

As we have seen, the Human Rights and Peace-Building agendas could be seen as overlapping. Of course there are also areas that do not overlap between the two agendas.

It is true that human rights and peace-building deal with the same reality and often the same social situation. The difference between the two traditions does not come from this, but from their moral and thematic roots when dealing with unjust and violent situations.

---

2. Article 1, *Universal Declaration of Human Rights.*

FIGURE 1: Areas of Overlapping Agendas

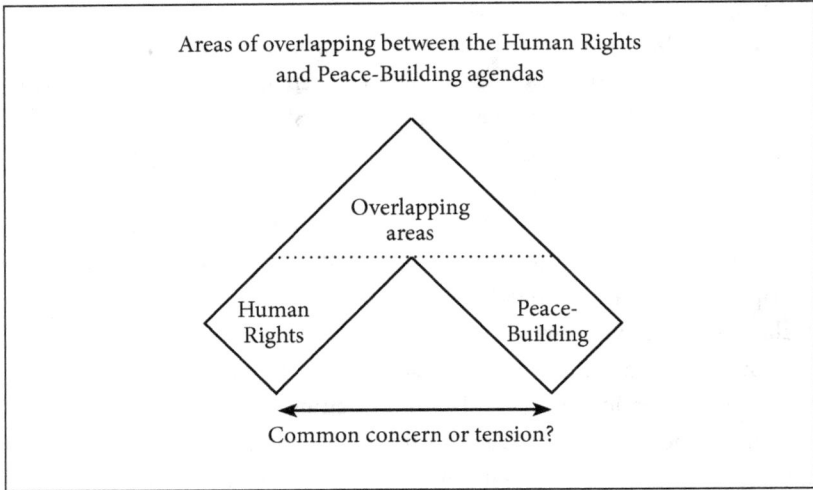

Areas of overlapping between the Human Rights and Peace-Building agendas

Overlapping areas

Human Rights

Peace-Building

Common concern or tension?

While the human rights system can refer to a number of "defining documents" of different dates (the majority of which are not older than a century) and with varying degrees of scope and legal and moral strength, the peace-building tradition has taken on different shapes over many centuries. Most important, the latter is not based on legal or otherwise legally binding texts, but on a commitment to moral principles with political and sometimes personal implications. It has both religious and secular roots, which sometimes are transformed into a state-based philosophy, for instance of just war, as well as into positions of pacifism, anti-militarism, or support of non-violent action.

POWER AND GENDER-RELATED THEMES

A few concepts do not lend themselves to be limited into either a peace-building or human rights context, nor to a specific level—be it individual or group (community, national, international). They cross such boundaries. There are two of these concepts that will follow us throughout this study and grow into thematic necessities in the analysis. One is a *power-related theme*. Since humanitarian disasters, protracted and violent conflicts, and military dictatorships are failures not only for the parties involved but for the international community as a whole, every conflict involves a power dimension between different actors.

In the Peace-Building agenda this may be exemplified by attempts as early as possible to get the parties to stop fighting and start negotiating. There are good reasons for this, it may save lives and make a conflict less entrenched. This inevitably results, however, in a situation where none of the parties is defeated militarily. Instead, negotiating in such early stages is one option among many and a continuation of fighting may be the chosen outcome or option. Early negotiations may even be seen as a useful break for recuperation and rearming of forces. Thus, negotiations and peace processes that take place between parties who *de facto* have other options than a peace commitment or surrender, are guided by an "egoistic" principle of self-protection for the party/group and its leaders as long as alternatives are possible. Not seldom the idea of negotiating parties is that the power remains in their hands and should be transformed into political and legal gains, i.e., protection from prosecution and a restoration of maximum and unimpeded political influence. As the quotation in the beginning of this chapter alludes to: is a dirty compromise acceptable?

The human rights system both relies upon and gives power to the state. It is the state as the duty-bearer that fulfills and protects rights and even controls their implementation. It is very much a self-ruling system giving control and power to the state. In a situation of war, the parties involved—whether the state or other parties acting without the control of a responsible government—can easily use their power structures at the expense of the rights holders and individuals being violated.

A second theme is *gender-related*. It is important throughout this study, not least due to the fact that in most military conflicts and wars women, as well as children, make up a majority of the civilians affected. This is not just about a lack of implementation or a violation of the Human Rights agenda. It is a wider phenomenon affecting all classes and ages in certain war situations. In addition, the reality in many violent conflicts is that sexual violence against women is used as a tool of warfare. Women are ultimately killed under such circumstances, but those surviving are nevertheless harmed in many ways, including physically and socially, as they often are stigmatized and marginalized. Therefore, a reconstruction of lives and societies has to be gender-based in its many forms—from local community relations to national policy initiatives.

In a gender analysis power is a critical component. The two concepts are closely related. When one man beats his wife it is direct violence, and when all men beat their wives it is not only direct violence but also structural violence if it is part of a behavioral pattern that is institutionalized through norms and actions. This qualitative change of the type of violence, when repeated and legitimized, is identified by cross-category relevant concepts. They make it impossible to reduce violence—between the sexes, in domestic life, in schools, in religious institutions, in work life or in the entertainment industry—to a one-time event, but reveal structural injustices and oppression practiced in particular places under guise of tradition, values, and necessities. Gender is one of the critical concepts.

The two concepts of power and gender meet at various critical points: in peace processes, development priority discussions, conflict prevention initiatives and, maybe more than elsewhere, post-conflict transitional issues. For these reasons, the relationship between human rights and peace, and therefore also peace-building, is a "work in progress" where the two concepts can develop new and innovative forms of cooperation rather than digging trenches in the midst of situations that more than anything need bridges.

THE UNITED NATIONS

The United Nations was designed as an instrument for peace from its very beginning in 1945. Human rights is reflected in the Charter of the United Nations and the Universal Declaration of Human Rights was adopted in 1948. At that time, human rights were considered a largely internal matter for the UN member states.

A UN High Commissioner for Refugees (UNHCR) was created in 1950, however it was not until 1994 that the position of UN High Commissioner for Human Rights (UNHCHR) was established. While the UN Department of Political Affairs (UNDPA) represents a long-standing political/diplomatic tradition of the UN system, the Office of the High Commissioner for Human Rights (OHCHR) represents a different and more distinct agenda. These two are supposed to act in a concerted way in order to effectively promote the values of the United Nations. This, however, is not always so.

Professor Hurst Hannum describes and analyses the tensions between UNDPA and OHCHR by studying their work in some selected contemporary conflict and peace processes. His first observation is that "violence or civil war *per se* does not necessarily violate international human rights norms."[3] Human rights law "has never had the lofty aim of ending all war," according to Hannum.[4] From this point of departure, writes Hannum, human rights law is therefore applicable in all situations, including war or armed conflict, terrorist attacks, and guerrilla warfare situations. While governments and government institutions are supposed to be the main protectors of human rights, the problem for human rights advocates in times of conflict is that "they assume the functionality of the very institutions that peace implementation operations are tasked to help bring into existence."[5] Or, as a human rights official working in Angola stated:

> The objective for human rights interventionists is to improve the situations they encounter, rather than simply denouncing them. Nonetheless, for most human rights activists, working with a government is heresy.[6]

There seems to be a cynical treatment of human rights in times of conflict: the agencies supposed to protect human rights become the violators themselves.

There are ways out if this dilemma, and Hannum presents approaches for dealing with it. His first observation is that:

> Promoting and protecting human rights during conflicts and immediately after their settlement in so-called "failed" or quasi-failed states is qualitatively different from promoting and protecting human rights in functioning states, even when the latter are suffering from serious violence (e.g., Northern Ireland, the Kurdish region of Turkey, and Colombia).[7]

From this starting point, Hannum uses the observation by the former Special Representative of the Secretary-General, Lakhtar Brahimi, who stated that:

> [Peacekeeping is becoming more difficult because] our expectations and agendas are not getting any more realistic. Instead, they have become more ambiguous and multifaceted, seeking to promote justice, national reconciliation, human rights, gender

3. Hannum, "Human Rights in Conflict Resolution," 5.
4. Ibid.
5. Putnam, quoted in ibid., 6.
6. Hannum, "Human Rights in Conflict Resolution," 6 n. 10.
7. Ibid., 7.

> equality, the rule of law, sustainable economic development and
> democracy—all at the same time, from day one, now, immedi-
> ately, even in the midst of conflict.[8]

Given that the conditions under which human rights should be implemented may be quite different, for instance in "failed states," and that it
also is naïve to believe in a quick realization of a major social change in a
society that even before the conflict was not close to such standards, pre-
pares for a more humble and therefore realistic approach. This is summarized in a view that Hannum shares with Christine Bell that peace
agreements "may be viewed as 'transitional' documents, that will give
way to more permanent arrangements once peace takes hold."[9]

The question is not about being dogmatic, but rather to be effective in the application of human rights norms in a society where "all"
norms are under threat and undermined. To establish a foundation for
the implementation of an emerging human rights normative system is
then a priority. Few human rights are absolute, states Hannum, and he
notes that most may be limited by other legitimate concerns of government, such as the protection of the rights of others, the maintenance of
public order or national security. While this possibility is often abused
by repressive regimes, and while they also require certain "procedural
requirements,"[10] limitations might be "more acceptable (or even more
desirable) than if a government attempted to impose the same limitations in a stable, democratic, peaceful state," according to Hannum.[11]

Finally, Hannum encourages the OHCHR to use its authority in a
responsible way. The OHCHR is not a Non-Governmental Organization
(NGO), it has a different mandate for its actions and therefore, according
to Hannum, it should be able to work both with sticks and carrots, if
necessary. In doing so, the Office should:

> . . . accept the challenge of the so-called realists in DPA and else-
> where and be prepared to defend its human rights positions not
> just by arguing that they are right but also by demonstrating that
> they are effective.[12]

8. Ibid., 48.

9. Ibid., 49; Bell, *Peace Agreements and Human Rights*, 9.

10. Hannum, "Human Rights in Conflict Resolution," 49 n. 124.

11. Ibid., 49.

12. Ibid., 50.

What Hannum identifies is both a certain tension in the UN system between the two agendas and possible principles for dealing with it. The agenda issues are the same for other organizations or states, but the practical implications—including how to deal with them—may differ between the UN, with its very special international role, and national and local NGOs, as well as for the civil society at large.

The United Nations is particularly exposed to the conflicting interests of the two agendas, since the organization in itself contains and represents both traditions. Hannum analyses how the UN deals with this. In his study of the promotion of human rights, peace, and security by the UNDPA and OHCHR, he shows how "the left hand does not know what the right hand does." Each of them represents the two agendas but work in relative isolation and with a certain lack of mutual understanding.

NATIONAL AND REGIONAL ORGANIZATIONS

The Organization for Economic Co-Operation and Development (OECD) has established a Joint Working Group on Human Rights and Conflict in order to study the present-day interface between "human rights" and "conflict" among policymakers, mediators, and diplomats, in relation to human rights advocates, through studying donor documents. At the time of writing, a report has not yet been published from the Joint Working Group on human rights and conflict.

A study by Elisabet Abiri is both an inventory of some positions in the debate and a proposal for a way out of the dilemma. She suggests in this respect that the conceptual basis for development cooperation policies could be changed into a uniform use of a human rights-based language. This would be a way to settle the dilemma, but at the expense of a peace-building approach.

Even if it is clearly stated that both fields have their own strength and are very much treated as two separate agendas, there is a stress to promote the idea of integrating human rights concerns into peace-building. That implies that human rights are looked upon as supporting peace-building while at the same time encouraging a more effective linkage. The duty is still there—if possible—to link the two agendas into one agenda, or at least to make human rights and peace objectives mainstream with a focus on "nodes."

The International Council on Human Rights Policy, in Switzerland, published in 2006 a report dealing with the place of human rights in peace agreements. The report addresses whether human rights provisions assist or hinder the search for peace by drawing on recent peace agreements, such as those in Cambodia, El Salvador, Mozambique, Bosnia and Herzegovina, Guatemala, Northern Ireland, Sierra Leone, and Burundi. More specifically, the report aimed at answering questions like: What human rights protections were provided for in the peace agreement? How did the peace agreement provide for these to be achieved in practice? Why did the parties agree to human rights protection?[13] The observation is that among other things "human rights frameworks and mechanisms to implement them are very often included in peace agreements" because "human rights frameworks emerge as an attempt to curtail or limit the manifestations of violent conflict, and also because they address core causes of conflict."[14] But it is also stated that "the role and acceptance of human rights is understood differently by parties to the conflict."[15] Two of the general recommendations in the report are:

> Human rights measures should be considered as a potential tool for limiting the conflict and building confidence at the pre-negotiation stage of an agreement. . . .
> Human rights frameworks aimed at current and future protection should be included or reinforced in peace agreements.[16]

There are some thematic issues that are both complimentary and in tension with human rights and conflict resolution. Such issues are refugees, displaced people and forcible dispossession of land and property.[17] The report states that dealing with the past in relation to questions of accountability and amnesty undoubtedly includes a dilemma for proponents of human rights and conflict resolution.[18] In its conclusion the report states that the approach of peace agreements might be:

> . . . concentrating on immediate delivery of basic human rights with temporary measures of immediate international monitor-

---

13. Bell, *Negotiating Justice?* 21.
14. Ibid., 38.
15. Ibid., 39.
16. Ibid., 48.
17. Ibid., 55.
18. Ibid., 80.

ing and enforcement if necessary, together with a road map for
institution-building and legal reform.[19]

The study by the International Council on Human Rights Policy has the
ambition to analyze the processes both before and after a peace agreement is signed. The inclusion of human rights provisions in peace agreements is a sign of awareness among both mediators (when relevant)
and negotiating parties. In the analysis, however, the concept of "peace"
sometimes refers to the "peace agreement," sometimes to a situation
emerging in the process and sometimes to developments after a peace
agreement is signed. This creates somewhat unclear conclusions in the
report, which nevertheless contains a number of useful discussions.

ACADEMIC RESEARCH

While it is appropriate to understand the millennia-old roots behind
"peace" and "human rights," we must at the same time recognize that
the linkage between them—both theoretically and practically—is still
under investigation. Some voices would, in addition to this, claim that
the whole debate is a theme of Western luxury, while those that live and
work in conditions lacking any trace of both human rights and peace
can easily see how closely linked they are.

A debate in the academic and policymaking communities that re-
ceived international attention at the time of its publication, and which
also has spurred further research in the field, is that between Felice Gaer
and an anonymous disputant in *Human Rights Quarterly* 1996/1997.[20]
Today, the debate is much wider than this early example reflects, but it is
nevertheless a good illustration of the dilemma: whatever road is taken,
there are problems over the implications that each tradition, i.e., each
agenda, formulates.

In the article from 1996 the international human rights community
was criticized by an anonymous author (and negotiator) for being in-
sensitive to the political consequences of its pressure for the integration
of human rights components in the negotiations and peace agreement

19. Ibid., 117.

20. See Anonymous, "Human Rights in Peace Negotiations"; and Gaer, "Reflections
on Human Rights Abuses."

in the conflict of former Yugoslavia. As is well known, the negotiation process took many turns and consisted of many initiatives and plans.[21]

The view of the author of the article, who was allowed to remain anonymous due to the sensitivity of the issue and the author's role in the negotiations, included criticisms of a statement by the prosecutor of the International Criminal Tribunal for the former Yugoslavia, Judge Richard Goldstone, who according to the author was irresponsible since he "would not be deterred by delicate negotiations to reach a lasting peace deal." Instead the Tribunal would maintain, according to the author's quotation of Goldstone, that "we are interested in building a body of legal evidence regardless of the political consequences." The author comments on this statement saying that:

> This surely must be wrong as a policy. What if the consequences of such a stance were the breakdown of the peace talks and thousands more would die in further conflict, in the name of what moral principle would one be able to defend those deaths?[22]

Gaer replies in the next issue of *Human Rights Quarterly* and she argues that it was the lack of clout from the international community (in particular the EU) that prolonged the war, rather than the commitment and advocacy of human rights advocates, including Judge Goldstone.

The debate referred to above was a precursor to a larger theme of research on overlapping and conflicting "ambitions" of the Human Rights and Peace-Building agendas in years to come. This is not the place for an overview of the research field as a whole, but a few major studies can illustrate some of the key issues of the debate.[23]

In a study from 2000, Christine Bell addresses the role of human rights in peace agreements and their relationship to international law, and therefore touches the subject of this study. She does not, however, penetrate the consequences for the peace process of the overlapping

21. The Dayton Peace Accords, from 1995, was the last in a series of attempts to reach an agreement in the Yugoslav conflict. Beginning in 1991 the European Community (EC) established different groups with the task of finding a solution, for instance the Carrington Conference and the Badinter Commission. In mid-1992 the United Nations and the EC organised the "London Conference on the Former Yugoslavia," which in practice became a series of conferences resulting in proposals such as the January 1993 "Vance-Owen Plan," the September 1993 "Invincible Plan," and the November 1993 "European Union Plan." None of them could effectively end the conflict.

22. Anonymous, "Human Rights in Peace Negotiations," 249ff.

23. This section is based on Nordquist, *Crossroads*, 15 ff.

agendas. Her research can be seen as a framework for the analysis of the relationship between human rights and peace agreements in various aspects. A major point in Bell's study is that peace agreements are regarded as "transitional constitutions," and she argues that "human rights provisions must be understood as an integral part of the constitution and as having particular transitional functions."[24] She also makes the observation that international law "is moving towards an increased notion of individual accountability and punishment during and after conflict."[25]

Bell is the main author of *Negotiating Justice?: Human Rights and Peace Agreements* (a report mentioned above), published in 2006, which is a study that in its structure and approach reflects the theoretical framework of her work in 2000. The content analysis method applied does not, however, fully allow conclusions of this causal nature.

Bell's study from 2000—with its focus on legal and political dimensions—is nicely complemented by Ruti Teitel's work, which stays within a legal framework. Teitel argues that transitional justice provides "an *independent* potential for effecting transformative politics"[26] and stresses that the modern forms of repression, with their systemic character, "implies a recognition of the mix of individual and collective responsibility."[27] Teitel brings us then beyond the legal sphere and implicitly into the arena of the overlapping agendas: dealing with the past is not only a matter of individual responsibility, but the society—in part or whole—has to reestablish itself as a just order.

An interesting position, in this context, is developed by Michael Feher (1999), who argues that a transitional process from war to peace is to be compared to a "civilizational jump." This resembles, to some extent, an original or traditional law-of-war position where the period called "war-time" (defined through an official declaration of war) implied that different legal frameworks be applied for one's own soldiers. Feher's view implies that justice before the "jump" is a different kind of justice than after, and the same is the case with "reconciliation." In this way one cannot assume legal or moral perfection before that "jump," but only after.

At this point we can make the observation that there is not one single dimension along which all of these studies can be placed. In

24. Bell, *Peace Agreements and Human Rights*, 9.
25. Ibid., 285.
26. Teitel, *Transitional Justice*, 213 (italics original).
27. Ibid., 217.

addition to the principled view, besides a more pragmatic one, there are also positions referring to the need to separate "peace" (understood in practice as a cease-fire and an end of fighting) on the one hand and the full-fledged instrument for achieving human rights and legal justice on the other. From the overview above, we can choose views of four authors and let them be representatives of typical positions in this debate. This can then be summarized as follows.

FIGURE 2: Four Views in the Debate on Human Rights and Peace-Building

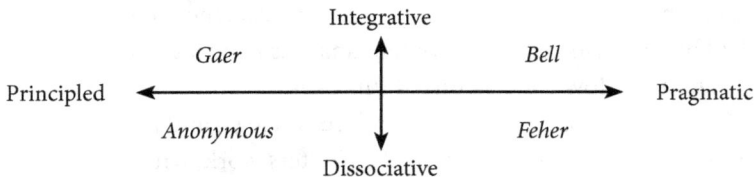

The *integrative* view regards international law and human rights, as far as law is concerned, on the one hand, and negotiations and peace processes, on the other, as one single process and thus they should be represented by one single, integrated document. This is one aspect of Gaer's response to the critique in the debate on the peace process in the Balkans. Bell takes a more *pragmatic* view in arguing that peace agreements are transitional documents and therefore human rights and international law provisions in this context need to be applied accordingly. This in practice often means adapting different instruments to different contexts in a way that alleviates a political solution that makes way for a more comprehensive legal and human rights application later. Finally, Feher argues for different agendas in times of war and peace: the transitional process means that a society makes a "jump of civilization" and thus reconciliation and justice are not the same before this jump and after. Therefore, for Feher one should *dissociate* and not integrate them into one single document, event, or process.

A substantial overview and contribution to this debate has been provided in Spanish from the Latin American horizon through the study of Iván Orozco, where he—rightly so—labels the dispute between the "doers of peace" and the "defenders of human rights" as a "family dispute."[28] Departing from the Latin American experience of dictator-

---

28. Orozco, *Sobre los Límites*, 318.

ships and self-imposed amnesties, Orozco brings up the convergence in Europe between human rights defenders and the peace movement during the last decade of the Iron Curtain. However, he argues that through the wars of Cambodia, former Yugoslavia, Rwanda, and elsewhere the tension within "the humanitarian family" became all the more visible. Orozco identifies the tension of politicians" versus "lawyers" as representing one conflict dimension. A second dimension is between "pragmatics" and "purists." The third is between "the managers of conflict" and "the democratizers." Orozco argues for a balance between the two agendas, but ends his discussion in the midst of debating the situation current in Colombia in of early 2005, without really stating a final position on the "family dispute."

Finally, Rodrigo Uprimny identifies in a useful way the gradual shift that different cases of transition from war to peace illustrate—from the legacy of Nuremburg and similar cases of *imposed justice,* to cases of a strong reconciliatory approach to the dilemma, which is the focus of this project. Also, according to Uprimny, Nuremburg and Bosnia represent *imposed justice,* while Argentina and Chile are cases of *self-amnesty* by the incumbent military governments. In Central America, on the other hand, it is possible to talk about *reciprocal pardons,* while South Africa, Uruguay, and Northern Ireland represent cases of *democratically legitimate* transitions.[29] While these cases are not the object of study in this project, there are certainly actors and movements in the countries discussed that have struggled with the dilemma of human rights and peace-building.

CIVIL SOCIETY ORGANIZATIONS

The adoption of the Universal Declaration of Human Rights in 1948 by the then newly formed United Nations was a significant and parallel development to the formation of a developed international normative framework as expressed in the Charter of the UN itself. While the UN Charter is based on states, the Universal Declaration addresses individuals irrespective of their state affiliation. These two developments—with their different formal standing—set a pattern for commitments and developments that both states and the civil society can utilize and address, from their respective points of departure.

---

29. *¿Justicia Transicional sin Transición?*, 33.

The monitoring of human rights has been a classic civil society agenda, partly in relation to the UN system, but more importantly in relation to the main duty-bearers, the constituent states. A number of human rights organizations, international and national, have over the years developed a monitoring capacity that is on a par with what governments and International Governmental Organizations (IGO) can produce.

In the civil society, different strands of civil organizations have over recent decades cooperated in developing a peace-building agenda in which these organizations have developed significant competence. Their roots and commitments may be based in different traditions—pacifist, labor, religious, humanitarian—but they meet in a concern for society, more than the state, and for the social more than the legal.

The end of the Cold War coincided with a radical increase of Non-Governmental Organizations (NGOs) in the Third World. Additionally new international organizations were formed, some of them specifically as human rights organizations, others were humanitarian or peace-building organizations. Examples of these human rights organizations include Human Rights Watch, Amnesty International, Helsinki Committee (Civil Rights Defenders) as well as the International Red Cross, with its special position. The peace-building side includes International Alert, Accord (South Africa), and Conciliation Resources. Numerous national organizations—often larger and regionally more influential than the ones mentioned here—are typical representatives of the two agendas.

These organizations are complex and address a wide range of issues, something that involves the use of different agendas, for different purposes. Some NGOs function similarly to the United Nations with different desks, or departments, to work on the basis of different agendas. Internally this may naturally cause problems and it also means that in relation to partner organizations in the field policies or directions from the same headquarters can have contradictory implications.

In the same way as individual organizations can cooperate in the field, through strategic or practical—or both—initiatives, the same is of course possible within an organization. This is a matter of structure, not of principle. On the general level, organizations might like to converge and integrate the two agendas—which is fine—and then be confronted with issues that lend themselves towards rather generalized formulations, as a solution to seemingly irreconcilable agendas. Thus, the strategic, project-oriented approaches discussed here could be an internal way of working for an organization, as well, and not only for agenda-specialized NGOs.

THE FOCUS OF THIS STUDY

Human rights and peace-building may be looked upon as two perspectives for enhancing the same goal and as necessarily being seen as complementary. When our study puts an "and" between human rights and peace-building it is an expression of the hypothesis that the concepts are not only interrelated but aiming at the same fundamental values.

It is also possible to formulate questions, often expressed by actors and organizations in a post-conflict situation, addressing the different positions but talking about one and the same situation:

> What does human rights and peace-building mean after systematic violations of human rights? Is the only acceptable road forward to let the process of legal justice have its course, taking its time to bring people into jail and after some years, probably, back to their village house and families? Or should the whole war period be exposed to common reflection among both victims and perpetrators, where truth telling and sharing not only becomes the victim's role but everyone's, so as to prepare for a mutual rebuilding process where legal justice is just one of many components?[30]

Given this background, the focus of this study is on describing and analyzing areas where the Human Rights and Peace-Building agendas, respectively, deal with the same reality and with the same goals (as described above) but do so with different purposes in mind. In addition, it will investigate possible ways and means to overcome and handle this tension, in different situations. Departing from how these agendas overlap in terms of commitment and proposals for action, the study will look at ways and approaches to converge and to make initiatives from both agendas more effective in different phases such as a conflict, post-conflict, and stabilization.

An "agenda" sets both the perspective and action—be it of government or international agencies, NGOs, or civil society groups. We will use the concept of "agenda" to summarize both theory and action among human rights organizations as well as peace-building organizations.

---

30. Nordquist, *Crossroads*, 1–2.

2

Human Rights and Peace-Building

HUMAN RIGHTS

THE CONCEPT OF HUMAN rights developed after the Second World War, although the roots may be traced further back in history. Human rights are basically used for describing the fundamental rights and freedoms for each and every human being. They are represented within a body of laws and legal documents that are founded on the principle of the inherent dignity of the human being and recognize the rights of all human beings to freedom, justice, and non-discrimination. Human rights are basically the agreed-upon consensus over the minimum standards for individuals to enjoy a life in dignity. At the same time they represent the dynamic framework involved in the process of interpreting new situations. These rights, as agreed upon by the states and accompanied by a will of the states to implement them, may be considered as a universal framework, though not all conventions are ratified by all states.

In principle, through the agreed-upon rights, each and every person will have the same rights in relation to the state and should be protected against the state's abuses and excesses of power as well as be protected against abuse performed by other actors in the society.

Basics on Human Rights

The foundation of human rights, according to the *Universal Declaration of Human Rights*, is based on the belief that "all human beings are born free and equal in dignity and rights" (Article 1). The declaration is today the foundational document concerning human rights. The principles of the declaration have over the years been accepted by the UN member states which thereby have recognized that the rights should be respected. The World Conference on Human Rights, held in Vienna in June 1993 and comprising 171 member states, by acclamation urged the universal ratification of human rights treaties and reaffirmed:

> . . . the solemn commitment of all States to fulfill their obligations to promote universal respect for, and observance and protection of, all human rights and fundamental freedoms for all in accordance with the Charter of the United Nations, other instruments relating to human rights, and international law. The universal nature of these rights and freedoms is beyond question.[1]

The International Bill of Human Rights consists of the declaration together with the two main covenants and other core human rights instruments:

- *International Covenant on Economic, Social and Cultural Rights*, adopted 1966 and entered into force 1976.

- *International Covenant on Civil and Political Rights*, adopted 1966 and entered into force 1976, with two optional protocols, the second aiming at the abolition of the death penalty.

- *International Convention on the Elimination of All Forms of Racial Discrimination*, adopted 1965 and entered into force 1969.

- *Convention on the Elimination of All Forms of Discrimination against Women*, adopted 1979 and entered into force 1981.

- *Convention against Torture and Other Cruel, Inhuman or Degrading Treatment or Punishment*, adopted 1984 and entered into force 1987.

- *Convention on the Rights of the Child*, adopted 1989 and entered into force 1990. Important optional protocols are *Optional Protocol to the Convention on the Rights of the Child on the Involvement of Children in Armed Conflict*, and *Optional Protocol to the Convention on the Rights of the Child on the Sale of Children, Child Prostitution and Child Pornography*, both adopted 2000 and entered into force 2002.

---

1. *Vienna Declaration and Programme of Action*, I:1.

- *International Convention on the Protection of the Rights of All Migrant Workers and Members of Their Families*, adopted 1990 and entered into force 2003.

- *International Convention for the Protection of All Persons from Enforced Disappearance*, adopted 2006.

- *Convention on the Rights of Persons with Disabilities*, adopted 2006 and entered into force 2008.

In connection with the conventions and the overall UN work with human rights there are several supervising committees, councils, and tribunals. These bodies are gaining more and more importance for the interpretation of the rules as well as for supervising the implementation made by the states subscribing to the conventions.

Here another resolution can also be mentioned from the UN Security Council dealing specifically with women and girls in armed conflict from different perspectives: as groups particularly exposed to violence in all forms, but also as peace-builders and strategic contributors to peace processes. In resolution 1325 (2000) the Security Council:

> *Calls on* all actors involved, when negotiating and implementing peace agreements, to adopt a gender perspective . . .

> *Calls upon* all parties to armed conflict to respect fully international law applicable to the rights and protection of women and girls, especially as civilians . . .

> *Calls on* all parties to armed conflict to take special measures to protect women and girls from gender-based violence, particularly rape and other forms of sexual abuse, and all other forms of violence in situations of armed conflict.

In the International Bill of Human Rights there are also regional frameworks such as the *African [Banjul] Charter on Human and Peoples' Rights*, the *American Convention on Human Rights*, and the *European Convention on Human Rights and Fundamental Freedoms*.

Unfortunately, human rights violations seem to be the norm in many countries. According to the subscription to human rights, the states of the world are considered to be of good will and in favor of implementing rights for their peoples. Yet, we know it is not always as simple as that, since there is still human vulnerability, discrimination (gender-based or otherwise), as well as misuse of power and unequal distribution of resources. At the same time, there seems to be no other effective alternative to states for universally trying to protect all human beings.

Human rights seek respect for the human dignity of each and every individual as human beings. To become part of a better society each human being needs to be guaranteed rights and protected against abuse and violations. This includes civil and political rights as well as economic, social, and cultural rights.[2]

Human rights are claimed to be *indivisible* and to have equal status, and cannot be positioned in a hierarchical order. In addition, human rights should be regarded as *interdependent* in relation to each other. No single human right can be treated, or protected, in isolation from others. This connection between different human rights is also underlined by the view that they are *interrelated,* which aims at describing that they all are in a relationship with one another. Finally, they are *universal,* which indicates the principle that human rights always are valid for, and apply equally to, all human beings.

A HUMAN RIGHTS–BASED APPROACH

There is no single definition of a "human rights–based approach," however there are several different indicators for purporting such an approach. It may be in relation to development and aid work[3], for instance in relation to a certain specific right such as equality[4] or the rights of the child[5].

All interplay between human beings includes power relations, not the least when it is about the state and the individual. A human rights–based approach looks upon power relations and power structures through a specific perspective distributing different key roles to participants called rights holders (mainly the individual) and duty bearers (mainly the state). Focusing on a human rights–based approach will indicate that the human being shall demand her/his rights. The rights are not given based on the good will of the state or based on needs but purely as rights in themselves.

2. For a list of human rights see for example Landman et al. (for the UNDP), *Indicators for Human Rights.*

3. See *Report: The Second Interagency,* and Hansén et al., *I rätt riktning.*

4. Goonesekere, *Rights-Based Approach.*

5. Theis, *Rights-Based Monitoring.*

From a legal point of view, human rights regulate the relationship between the individual and the state, giving the state a duty of protecting each person. In a normal situation there seems to be reason to believe that human rights function very often, however they are threatened, for instance, during war and violent conflict. Duty bearers, having human rights obligations, can in some cases also be international organizations or individuals, for example parents in relation to their children. But the state remains the primary duty bearer. At the same time rights holders may not always be individuals but in some circumstances groups, such as indigenous peoples.[6]

FIGURE 3: A Human Rights-Based Approach

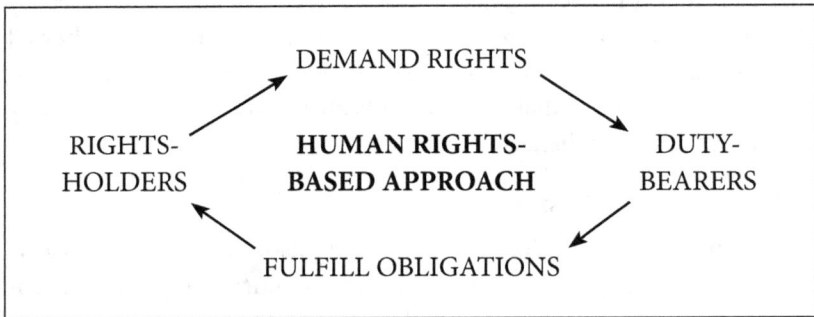

DEMAND RIGHTS

RIGHTS-HOLDERS   **HUMAN RIGHTS-BASED APPROACH**   DUTY-BEARERS

FULFILL OBLIGATIONS

All this is based on the premises that the rights holders as well as the duty bearers are aware of their respective rights and duties. A human rights–based approach places the human being as the central subject and as a rights holder. One crucial step in a human rights–based approach is a focus on identifying rights holders (especially the most marginalized and discriminated against) and duty bearers (the states' obligations) in a society and the relationship between them. Since the rights of each individual is dependent on the conviction that each and every human being possesses the same rights, a human rights–based approach builds on a broad participation and a kind of "popular" awareness through citizen participation. The rights holders cannot be passive and it is about who is in power and in control. As Professor Abdullahi Ahmed An-Na'im puts it:

6. See *Indigenous and Tribal Peoples Convention.*

> Since we cannot be anywhere else (than our own "home" loca-
> tion) long enough, with sufficient resources, understanding of
> the local situation, and ability to achieve sustainable change, the
> best we can do is to invest in empowering local actors to protect
> their own rights.[7]

The implication is that human rights claims are often more effective when people act together as a group. Even if human rights are basically an issue for the individual person being violated against, civil society, including NGOs, can play an important role for upholding and claiming these rights. Civil society can, for instance, monitor violations against human rights, influence states to better promote human rights, and support individuals or groups demanding their rights. Thus human rights determine the relationship between, on the one hand, individuals and groups with valid claims and, on the other hand, the state and non-state actors. This gives the civil society a role of demanding the duty bearers to implement human rights in four fundamental ways, illustrated by the following four concepts: *respect* (for all human beings and abstaining from all violations), *promote* (without discrimination and with gender equality), *defend* (all rights and freedoms), and *fulfill* (through appropriate action).

Strategies and goals concerning human rights are focused on a process of respecting, protecting, and fulfilling normative human rights. Civil and political rights along with economic, social, and cultural rights are of course crucial for all human rights activities. The following scheme explains the different duties of the state in relation to human rights categories.[8]

---

7. An-Na'im, "Towards," 34.
8. Based on *Indicators for Human Rights*.

TABLE 1: Goals and Strategies Concerning Human Rights

	Respect (no interference in the exercise of the right)	**Protect** (prevent violations from third parties)	**Fulfill** (provision of resour-ces and the outcomes of policies)
Civil and Political Rights	Measures to prevent state actors from committing torture, extra-judicial kill-ing, disappearances, arbitrary detention, unfair trials, elector-al intimidation, and disenfranchisement.	Measures to prevent non-state actors from committing violations, such as torture, extra-judicial killings, disappearances, abduction, and elec-toral intimidation.	Investment in judiciaries, prisons, police forces, elec-tions, and resource allocations to ability.
Economic, Social, and Cultural Rights	Measures to prevent state actors from committing ethnic, racial, gender or linguistic discrimi-nation in health, education, and welfare and resource allocations below ability.	Measures to prevent non-state actors from engaging in discriminatory behavior that limits access to health, education, and other welfare.	Progressive realiza-tion. Investment in health, education, and welfare, and resource allocations to ability.

All rights—civil and political as well as economic, social, and cultural—are in their entirety worth fighting for. At the same time a human rights–based approach makes fundamental priorities by focusing on the marginalized, non-privileged, and excluded groups in a society. Those may take different shape in different settings and countries. In a global setting it may also be a question of relations between the South and the North in the struggle for reducing poverty and hunger in the world. The priority is very much about human beings forced into powerlessness and who therefore lack control over their situation. In addition, in many oc-casions it is striking that those who are marginalized and powerless are women.

The importance of focusing on the most vulnerable and excluded in a society is underscored in the *Vienna Declaration*:

Great importance must be given to the promotion and protection of the human rights of persons belonging to groups which
have been rendered vulnerable, including migrant workers, the
elimination of all forms of discrimination against them, and the
strengthening and more effective implementation of existing human rights instruments. States have an obligation to create and
maintain adequate measures at the national level, in particular in
the fields of education, health and social support, for the promotion and protection of the rights of persons in vulnerable sectors of their populations and to ensure the participation of those
among them who are interested in finding a solution to their own
problems.[9]

A human rights-based approach also prioritizes non-discrimination.
This includes identifying and proving discrimination, as well as prevent-
ing discrimination and marginalization. In many cases, each and every
person exposed to a violation of their human rights and/or discrimination belongs to a particular minority or group that is based on ethnicity,
religion, color, HIV status, or economical marginalization.

When talking about a rights–based approach to development, the
former UN Secretary-General, Kofi Annan, declared:

A rights-based approach to development describes situations
not simply in terms of human needs, or of developmental requirements, but in terms of society's obligations to respond to
the inalienable rights of individuals. It empowers people to demand justice as a right, not as charity, and gives communities a
moral basis from which to claim international assistance where
needed.[10]

International Humanitarian Law

"The laws of war" are regulated by the International Humanitarian Law,
which comes into force in a situation of war. These rules have been
developed under the leadership of the International Committee of the
Red Cross (ICRC). The four Geneva Conventions of 1949 are the main
treaties, together with their Additional Protocols.[11] The International

9. *Vienna Declaration*, I:24.

10. *Annual Report of the Secretary-General* (1998).

11. The full text of the Conventions and Protocols are available only from the ICRC
at http://www.icrc.org/ihl.nsf/CONVPRES?OpenView.

Humanitarian Law is a set of rules seeking to limit the effects of an armed conflict. The aim is to protect those not involved as direct combatants, such as the civil population, the wounded and sick, and prisoners of war.

There is a difference between international armed conflicts involving two or more states and non-international armed conflicts restricted to the territory of a single state. In the latter case a limited range of rules apply, both according to Common Article 3 (in the four Geneva Conventions) and the Additional Protocol II (1977) to the Conventions. Common Article 3 states:

> (1) Persons taking no active part in the hostilities, including members of armed forces who have laid down their arms and those placed hors de combat by sickness, wounds, detention, or any other cause, shall in all circumstances be treated humanely, without any adverse distinction founded on race, color, religion or faith, sex, birth or wealth, or any other similar criteria. To this end, the following acts are and shall remain prohibited at any time and in any place whatsoever with respect to the above-mentioned persons:
>
>> (a) violence to life and person, in particular murder of all kinds, mutilation, cruel treatment and torture;
>>
>> (b) taking of hostages;
>>
>> (c) outrages upon personal dignity, in particular humiliating and degrading treatment;
>>
>> (d) the passing of sentences and the carrying out of executions without previous judgment pronounced by a regularly constituted court, affording all the judicial guarantees which are recognized as indispensable by civilized peoples.
>
> (2) The wounded and sick shall be collected and cared for.

The International Humanitarian Law at the same time prohibits or restricts certain weapons and methods of warfare. Among the conventions can be mentioned:

1. *Convention on the Prohibition of the Development, Production and Stockpiling of Bacteriological (Biological) and Toxin Weapons and on Their Destruction (1972).*

2. *Convention on Certain Conventional Weapons* (1980), with five operative protocols.

3. *Convention on the Prohibition of the Development, Production, Stockpiling and Use of Chemical Weapons and on their Destruction* (1993).

4. *The Convention on the Prohibition of the Use, Stockpiling, Production and Transfer of Anti-Personnel Mines and on Their Destruction* (Ottawa Convention) (1997).

The Most Serious Crimes

Concerning the most serious crimes like war crimes, crimes against humanity, and genocide, there is a special body of treaties including both conventions and tribunals for the prosecution of persons responsible for genocide and other serious violations. Examples of such tribunals are the International Criminal Tribunal for Rwanda, the International Criminal Tribunal for the former Yugoslavia, and the International Criminal Court.

There are two main instruments warranting mention here:

1. *Convention on the Prevention and Punishment of the Crime of Genocide*, adopted 1948 and entered into force 1951.

2. *Rome Statute of the International Criminal Court*, adopted 1998 and entered into force 2002.

The convention from 1948 recognizes in the preamble that "at all periods of history genocide has inflicted great losses on humanity" and that "in order to liberate mankind from such an odious scourge, international co-operation is required." Article 2 presents a definition of genocide also named "the crime of crimes":

> In the present Convention, genocide means any of the following acts committed with intent to destroy, in whole or in part, a national, ethnical, racial or religious group, as such:
>
> (a) Killing members of the group;
>
> (b) Causing serious bodily or mental harm to members of the group;
>
> (c) Deliberately inflicting on the group conditions of life calculated to bring about its physical destruction in whole or in part;

(d) Imposing measures intended to prevent births within the group;

(e) Forcibly transferring children of the group to another group.

The *Rome Statute*, from 1998, regulates the jurisdiction of the permanent International Criminal Court. Article 5 deals with:

... the most serious crimes of concern to the international community as a whole. The Court has jurisdiction in accordance with this Statute with respect to the following crimes:

(a) The crime of genocide;

(b) Crimes against humanity;

(c) War crimes;

(d) The crime of aggression.

Crimes against humanity are identified as "committed as part of a widespread or systematic attack directed against any civilian population" and include among others: murder, extermination, enslavement, deportation or forcible transfer of population, torture, the crime of apartheid as well as "rape, sexual slavery, enforced prostitution or any other form of sexual violence of comparable gravity."

When national authorities are unable to protect their own population from those grave crimes or, even worse, when they take part in these crimes, the international community through the UN Security Council can decide upon the use of force to protect the population.

Ethnic cleansing must also be mentioned even if there is presently no legal definition of the concept. The term was used in the context of former Yugoslavia for activities with the aim of forcing an ethnic group away from an area thereby changing the composition of the population.

Peace According to Human Rights Instruments and the UN Charter

The Human Rights agenda, as formulated in the main body of UN declarations and conventions, do in some cases include the concept of peace and maintain a relationship between human rights and peace. In the preamble of the *Universal Declaration of Human Rights* (1948) the equal and inalienable rights are said to be the foundation of world peace as well as of freedom and justice.[12] While referring to the *Charter of the United Nations*, both the *Covenant on Civil and Political Rights* (1966) and the *Covenant on Economic, Social and Cultural Rights* (1966) make the same connection between rights and peace.[13] The *Convention on the Elimination of All Forms of Racial Discrimination* (1963) pinpoints discrimination based on race, color, or ethnic origin as obstacles to peaceful relations among nations and they are thereby a cause serious enough to disturb peace and security. The *Convention on the Elimination of All Forms of Discrimination against Women* (1979) affirms that the strengthening of international peace and security will contribute to the attainment of full equality between men and women as well as proclaiming that peace requires maximum participation of women on equal terms with men in all fields. It should also be mentioned that some of the UN documents state that education is crucial for the strengthening of respect for, among other important values, human rights, as well as the maintenance of peace.

Even if peace is rather rare as a concept in human rights treaties, it is basically stated that the rights are looked upon as a foundation for peace. It may also be concluded that violations against human rights, such as discrimination, are an obstacle to peace and also that peace will contribute to the fulfillment of human rights.

According to human rights principles, the human being oppressed and exposed to violations of her/his rights under tyranny does have options. The *Universal Declaration of Human Rights* states in the preamble:

> ... Whereas it is essential, if man is not to be compelled to have recourse, as a last resort, to rebellion against tyranny and oppression, that human rights should be protected by the rule of law.

Such a rebellion may easily escalate into an open violent conflict and such situations might appear simple based on a human rights–based approach. People rebelling are to be considered rights holders having been

12. "Whereas recognition of the inherent dignity and of the equal and inalienable rights of all members of the human family is the foundation of freedom, justice and peace in the world."

13. The same goes for the *Convention against Torture and Other Cruel, Inhuman or Degrading Treatment or Punishment* (1984), the *Convention on the Rights of the Child* (1989) and the *Convention on the Rights of Persons with Disabilities* (2006).

marginalized and/or discriminated against by a tyrannical duty bearer. The experiences tell that the distinction is not easy to uphold if rebellion has developed into an ongoing war. Both parties in an ongoing war expose themselves to the risk of committing violations against human rights and International Humanitarian Law. At the same time, the tyrant usually has the power structures and military resources that are increasingly responsible for the violations during the fight.

In a situation of violent conflict human rights are applicable to the same degree as in a non-violent or peaceful situation. There is nothing in the human rights instruments prohibiting war, but the demands of human rights should always be applied. The International Humanitarian Law takes the same position in situations of violent conflict and war, by not prohibiting war but regulating the conduct of war and the use of weapons. The regulations concerning the most serious crimes such as genocide, crimes against humanity, war crimes, and the crime of aggression place a limit on what is considered to be acceptable in a war and pinpoint what acts are considered to be liable for legal punishment of the perpetrators.

The relationship between human rights and peace was recognized in the UN International Conference on Human Rights in Teheran in 1968, which stated "that peace and justice are indispensable to the full realization of human rights" as well as that gross denials of human rights "endanger the foundations of freedom, justice and peace in the world."[14]

The final statement from the World Conference on Human Rights in Vienna 1993 says that the respect for, and observance of, human rights improve conditions for peace and security "in conformity with the Charter of the United Nations."[15] A classic interpretation of the relationship of human rights to peace is that:

> . . . peace can be safeguarded only as the result of domestic evolution in which human rights are implemented for everyone. Conversely, the realization of these rights will be possible only when, in the process of social and cultural transformation, the parties abstain from violence and negotiate their differences through participatory, democratic means. In this process, they

14. "Proclamation of Teheran."
15. *Vienna Declaration*, preamble.

should continuously refer to the Universal Declaration for guidance regarding the accommodations to be made.[16]

PEACE-BUILDING

The references to a connection between human rights and peace, as demonstrated in the quotations in the previous section, provide a good reason for investigating what "peace" and "peace-building" stand for and how they can be practiced.

The archipelago of concepts used to describe various phases and aspects of peace processes become larger and larger. The word "archipelago" is chosen deliberately here: these concepts do not necessarily relate to each other, and if they do, the nature of the relationship is not always defined or agreed upon.

For a long period, the concepts of peace processes dealt with the resolution, settlement, management, or mitigation of conflict. This was achieved through negotiation, mediation, arbitration, facilitation, or other forms of direct or third party involvement. However, once an agreement of some sort was achieved, this proved not to be sufficient—peace does not follow automatically from a "peace agreement." This insight brought a set of other concepts into the archipelago, such as early warning, conflict prevention, conflict pre-emption, and preventive diplomacy. In his report to the UN in 1992, entitled *An Agenda for Peace*, Secretary-General Boutros Boutros-Ghali outlines the difference between "making," "keeping," and "building" peace. To "make" peace is in his language to exert force in order to install, or impose, negative peace, i.e., to bring an end to violence between conflicting parties, outright oppression, and a lack of social order. To "keep" this peace is the second task, which means to maintain this first-level of often precarious peace, through, for instance, peace-keeping forces, a cease-fire that is monitored and verified, or through other agreements that make the parties more inclined to negotiate than fight. The third task is then to "build" peace, which means to replace the temporary arrangements of a cease-fire or a peace agreement, and possibly demobilization of soldiers, with institutions—such as police, legislation, and other services—that provide for maintaining a long-term basis for fundamental aspects of peace. This requires convincing people that democratic institutions could best serve their interests

16. Eide, "Article 28," 621.

in the long run. From this point it is also possible to develop a wider concept of peace than the first steps of peace-making would allow.

These three concepts illustrate stages in a peace process. They can also be summarized in the following way:

FIGURE 4: Three Stages in a Long-Term Peace Process

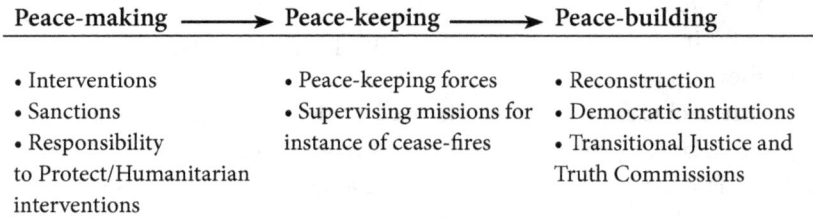

Peace-making ———▸ Peace-keeping ———▸ Peace-building

• Interventions	• Peace-keeping forces	• Reconstruction
• Sanctions	• Supervising missions for	• Democratic institutions
• Responsibility	instance of cease-fires	• Transitional Justice and
to Protect/Humanitarian		Truth Commissions
interventions		

Concepts of Peace

From the early 1990s the concepts of peace-making, peace-keeping, and peace-building entered the scene of international security and development policy formation. These concepts indicate that if peace—of some sort—should be achieved, it cannot rely on conflict prevention or other "negative" concepts. Instead, it has to be based on a constructive approach, i.e., on some fundamental commitments and mechanisms in a society. Without them, violence will recur no matter how good a peace agreement is in itself.

What these commitments and mechanisms are, and how they can be established, are important matters of focus for the concept of peace-building. We will not go into defining the concepts mentioned above in great detail, but will instead focus on the concept and practice of peace-building. In order to do that, two things are required: we need to know what "peace" is and what it means to "build" it.

The classic division of peace is that of a *negative* or a *narrow* peace—where peace means an absence of armed violence between or within states or communities. *Positive* or *wide* peace includes the narrow peace, plus justice and welfare among all citizens.[17] This division is still a useful way of identifying a qualitatively different way to talk about peace.

---

17. For a discussion on negative and positive peace, see Galtung, *Peace by Peaceful Means.*

Obviously, given the short-term perspective connected to establishing peace in the negative sense of the word, "negative peace" then would mean, for instance, that:

- there is no violence—not even sporadic—between groups or between the state and groups in a society;

- political issues are settled without threats or violence;

- state authorities, like police and the military, function without arbitrary beatings, arrests, or other threat-based methods of intimidation.

If only these narrow criteria of peace are realized, it creates a situation that profoundly changes the lives of many people. One does not need to turn to the concept of "wide peace" with its panorama of justice, equality, and welfare for all to find reasons for peace-building. Many reasons with equal strength can be based upon basic human rights such as the right to life, freedom of expression, and freedom from fear and arbitrary treatment. The narrow peace carries a great deal of human rights protection as well. These fundamental human rights illustrate that there are core values in a narrow, fundamental definition of peace.

The difference between *narrow* and *wide* peace should not be made into non-related approaches to development. In practice they relate to each other effectively. When the narrow peace is realized, it gives a natural basis to go further toward a concept of wider peace. "Peace-building" then—being a long-term undertaking in its nature—most often also means a possibility to establish peace in a more positive sense of the word: there is no end to what a wide peace can contain.

Solving Conflicts, Building Peace

In 2005, the then UN Secretary-General, Kofi Annan, noted in his report *In Larger Freedom: Towards Development, Security and Human Rights for All* that there was an institutional gap in the efforts of the UN between mediation and long-term development. The message was that "if we are going to prevent conflict we must ensure that peace agreements are implemented in a sustained and sustainable manner."[18] The Secretary-General proposed the creation of a UN Peacebuilding Commission (PBC) in order to address this gap. In 2007 the PBC commenced its work.

18. *Larger Freedom*, 31.

Besides the policy and lessons-learned dimensions of the commission's work, it has also established a peace-building fund.

The importance of the PBC is, for the moment at least, related to the recognition of the peace-building dimension in the process of moving from peace-making and basic stability to long-term development of peace with justice. Between these ends of a "stability continuum" there is room for approaches that recognize, for instance, the difference between a "post-conflict" situation and—for want of a better concept—a "development-prepared" situation.

A post-conflict situation has achieved the end to a dominating conflict—its issues and violent expressions—but may still have a number of minor issues remaining to be settled, which can result in flare-ups of violence, attempts by spoilers to undermine an agreement, etc. A development-prepared situation is stabilized on the level that some fundamental functions of the state and society are restored: there is capacity to facilitate cooperation and make credible long-term commitments while, at the same time, deal with day-to-day matters that always require attention.

In order to assist in the transformation of a society from a post-conflict state to a development-prepared situation, different types of peace-building initiatives are possible. The PBC today represents the most recent institutional recognition on the international level of the need for these types of initiatives. In the following we will develop in more detail what these initiatives may stand for.

Four Types of Peace-Building

Following the discussion from the 1990s to the present, peace-building has been widely described as any step towards a peaceful and lasting social structure irrespective of when during a peace process the step is taken. At the same time, it is generally agreed that peace-building has both a process-based dimension and an institutional dimension. A minimum common position seems to be that *peace-building means establishing processes as well as institutions that defend and promote security, justice, and welfare on a day-to-day basis.* This definition can be applied to the following four types of peace-building.

TABLE 2: Four Types of Peace-Building

	Process-based	Institutional
Short-term	peace negotiation, dialogue and awareness	cease-fire verification, demobilization
Long-term	reconciliation, reintegration, empowerment	police, justice, welfare system

SHORT-TERM AND PROCESS-BASED PEACE-BUILDING

The initiation of talks, or negotiations, between parties in conflict marks a qualitative shift in their relations, in the sense that it introduces a way of dealing with their conflicting demands that, until that point in time, was not considered a priority. This change, of course, does not mean that violence has stopped, or will stop. At the same time, negotiations are often connected to a temporary cessation of violence.

One of the most prominent early contributions to a peace process from the international community is the possibility it has to invite, organize, and prepare dialogue/talks/negotiations between parties who, without this assistance, would have found it difficult for political reasons to take the same initiative. These kinds of initiatives are not costly, neither practically or politically. They can be made with a low profile and require, more than anything else, trust among the parties. It is probably correct to say that it is at least as common, if not more so, for NGOs rather than governments to take these kinds of initiatives.

This is possible because most armed conflicts today are internal and in internal conflicts it is common that a wide array of actors are more or less directly involved. Often NGOs, local or international, have better access to local conditions and actors in a country than governments have during conflict. Here a double role is possible, whereby international NGOs can strengthen local NGOs so that they are able to contribute on their own terms to the development of peace in their country. International NGOs, on the other hand, can take initiatives that are not politically or practically possible for those acting locally.

While it is obvious that processes based on dialogue, mutual cooperation, and the mobilization of groups around a peace process can take a long time, these activities are still only a beginning of a much larger effort, which is reflected by the three other types of peace-building in Table 2. This should, however, not result in a rejection or reduction of the importance of the nature of the first contacts that are established between groups and individuals in a peace process. Failure to recognize this, perhaps because of the argument that one needs to get into the "hard stuff" early, can easily be counterproductive in the long run.

Thus we have identified both a structural and relational component in short-term, process-based peace-building. It is not difficult to understand the need for structure in a period of violence and war, and for trust in a period of animosity. This is what the short-term process can offer to the parties, along with their communities and the country.

LONG-TERM AND PROCESS-BASED PEACE-BUILDING

This insight leads us into the long-term processes that obviously have to work under very different conditions in comparison to the short-term processes. There are, for instance, no major peace agreements signed today that do not include a mechanism to deal with the dimension of reconciliation. In most cases this is an established part of a final or comprehensive peace agreement.

Long-term process-based peace-building faces many risks. A common pattern for so-called "truth and reconciliation commissions" is that they work intensively through a large number of different activities (hearings, historical investigations, statement-taking from witnesses, legal processes, reparations, symbolic acts, etc.) over a short time, so as to evade the risk of becoming hostage to political changes in the country or political actors that start to get cold feet in the face of the outcome of the commission's work. Nevertheless, reconciliation is a long-term process and a truth commission can only provide input at the beginning of such a process.

Additionally, funding and—if it has been there from the beginning—an international commitment is at risk in long-term processes. Donors seldom have the sustainability required for supporting long social processes.

Nevertheless, this kind of long-term, gradual, and committed process may turn out to be the most effective protection against recurring conflict in the long run. This is true for two reasons: first, the process is in itself a forum for dealing with unfinished matters in the peace process; and second, after a significant experience of mutual friction and friendship a confidence is established on a level that would not be possible to achieve through other means. In this way, a mechanism for conflict prevention is built into a society that has gone through this kind of long-term, process-based peace-building.

SHORT-TERM AND INSTITUTIONAL PEACE-BUILDING

It is often an immediate result from successful peace talks that troops—and the support functions for troops and armies—are halted. It becomes only a matter of time and a matter of practicality rather than one of principle, if and when the dismantling of the structures of guerillas, a scattered army, etc. is to be made. The international community has the capacity to monitor and verify such processes on relatively short notice, and it is—relatively speaking—one of the more uncontroversial parts of a peace process to fulfill this task. We shall not go into detail of this highly specialized and technical field. However, it deserves mention that in the middle of this seemingly hardcore type of activity there is a great deal of trust, commitment, and loyalty necessary between the experts and staff involved, including persons from the conflicting parties, for fulfilling activities such as monitoring and verification missions. Often they have to make an uncompleted peace agreement better as political negotiators do not always realize the complexities on the ground. Thus, without a proper level of trust on the political level, any verification of a cease-fire or demobilization process can go astray due to their complexity.

LONG-TERM AND INSTITUTIONAL PEACE-BUILDING

There is certainly a point in the argument where one "cannot sit talking" while killing goes on in the street—someone has to be "out there" safe-guarding law and order. While dialogue, recognition, and trust-building may be necessary for progress in the larger process, there needs to be a concrete system that takes care of day-to-day issues of immediate concern for a society. This means that there cannot only be a police force, but also a police academy that secures the long-term recruitment of officers; there cannot only be international peace-keeping troops, but maybe even a Security Sector Reform that establishes a new, functional army, police, and justice system.

This type of peace-building is the most recent component in "development cooperation." Still, social services, hospitals, education, and a welfare system on a national level are the traditional, but very vital, parts of such cooperation.

ORGANIZATIONAL AND RELATIONAL ASPECTS

Finally, in order to understand these four types of peace one has to recognize that each of the four types above have in addition both an *organizational* and a *relational* aspect. If we take the example of peace negotiations, we find that there is no negotiation without both political conditions and a structural setting for them. Yet at the same time, the individuals play a critical role for the final success of the negotiations. For all four types of peace-building we should recognize the necessary combination of both structures and human relations in order to understand their particular characteristics.

The *organizational* dimension of peace-building is probably the most analyzed and discussed. It concerns the (re-)establishment of societal institutions that can provide protection and security—sometimes as an immediate response to what is agreed in a peace agreement, or to what was a major issue in a conflict. While a structural response to conflict issues requires resources—both human and physical—it also presupposes the function of some fundamental political organs of the state.

The *relational* dimension of peace-building is—for obvious reasons—equally important, in comparison to the structural: without functioning human beings in a structure not much will happen, besides corruption perhaps. This aspect is more closely related to the process dimensions of peace-building, thus it is dependent on time and individuals' interest and ability to be part of such processes.

In conclusion, for the international community, in its cooperation and initiatives on different levels, the four different types of peace-building in Table 2 make up a set of fundamentally different approaches—the time dimension is definitively critical, and processes and structures/organizations are qualitatively different dimensions as well.

3

Case Studies of Five Countries

THERE IS SIGNIFICANT VARIATION in the conditions where human rights and peace-building efforts are implemented. Countries, regions, and local conditions vary to an extent that makes comparison difficult. In order to overcome this, and in order to illustrate how the two agendas—Human Rights and Peace-Building—are present in complicated realities, two recurrent perspectives are introduced for all the following cases as a basis for a comparative reading. These are, first, the dimension of *livelihood*—the conditions under which daily life is unfolding—and, second, the dimension of *confidence*—the trust that people have in their state administration and its political system, as well as in the local community. These two are described as a set of two separate "agendas of life conditions" in the five case studies analyzed below. Finally, we will also include an NGO perspective in order to illustrate how the perspective of NGOs can be expressed in that particular situation.

COLOMBIA

Colombia is the geographical centerpiece of the countries in Latin America who gained their independence in the early 1800s following wars of liberation, fought against Spanish colonial rule in the northern part of South America. Through these wars Venezuela, Colombia, Ecuador, Peru, and Panamá became independent within the span of a few decades.

Today, the concept of a "liberation war" can give a wrong impression, according to a participant in a seminar preparing this study in Colombia in 2007, since "liberation" may give the impression that the country was liberated from the rule of a few elite group families of landowners and, later on, industrialists, all of European—and in the case of Colombia, mostly Spanish—origin. But the concept refers to the liberation from the Spanish Crown, not from a particular social structure. Instead, this elite rule structure still marks the societies to this day.

The central actors in Colombian history since the nation's independence have been the landowners. This is so not only because of their economic role as providers of jobs, food, and other agricultural products, but also for their physical control of the land, the law, and social order that provide for their subsequent political influence and economic power. The impact of this social and economic structure is enhanced by the geographical location of Colombia in a mountainous region in northern South America, linking the Pacific with the Atlantic, something that in practice divides the country into a few relatively distinct and self-contained regions.[1]

Colombia today has a strong economy, according to traditional measures, with a growth in its GDP—before the global financial crisis—of over 4 percent during a 15-year period, outperformed in Latin America only by Chile. At the same time, the divide between rich and poor in the country has never been wider.

Politically, the ongoing internal armed conflict in Colombia became the most serious and longest internal war in South America after Guatemala signed a peace agreement in 1996 following a long process of negotiations. One of Colombia's guerilla groups, Revolutionary Armed Forces of Colombia (FARC), initiated its armed conflict in the 1960s. It and the smaller National Liberation Army (ELN) represent the two remaining leftist guerilla groups still fighting in the country.

This internal conflict has a death toll that amounts to some 3,000–4,000 casualties per year and has resulted in more than 3 million individuals being internally displaced[2] (a figure second only to Afghanistan), and has produced a long list of examples of "torture and other cruel, inhuman, or degrading treatment or punishment," as serious violations of human rights are defined by the international community.

A particular feature of the Colombian situation is the systematic and widespread taking of hostages, which in the case of FARC has reached 700 kidnappings at the time of this book being written and about 100 for ELN. Both organizations are presently listed as terrorist organizations by

---

1. Internal, post-independence wars in the 1800s in Colombia have been over the role of Bogotá, the capital, in comparison to the level of influence of the regions.

2. *2011 UNHCR Country Operations Profile—Colombia.*

the European Union and the United States. The Colombian government is also on the list of actors committing serious human rights violations in Colombia. In addition, the Colombian Armed Forces is repeatedly accused of having links or cooperating with paramilitary groups or other private armies.

There is no comprehensive peace process under way in Colombia of the kind we have seen, for instance, in Guatemala (see below) in the 1990s. A partial but important peace process took place in the early 1990s and ended with the signing of a new constitution in 1991 and the transformation of one of the major guerilla groups, M-19, which at the time was the second largest in the country, into a political party. Since then—and while the armed struggle of FARC and the ELN continued—paramilitary groups have emerged with both silent and sometimes an open support from the Colombian state. In the end, these groups—who were over ten in number—became in the early 2000s the most significant extra-judicial armed groups in Colombia, besides FARC, often acting in liaison with regional army commanders and defending the interests of local landholders and industrialists who were often, sometimes by coercion, financially backing them. In some years the paramilitary groups were responsible for a large majority of the massacres and extra-judicial killings that took place in Colombia.

The paramilitary groups never proclaimed war against the state, rather the opposite: in the absence of the state's ability to protect their landholdings against guerilla infiltration, the paramilitaries argued for their right to take up arms to defend these holdings. Over the years they started to finance their activities through the narcotics trade, as FARC had long done. In 2004, the United Self-Defense Forces of Colombia (AUC) started a self-initiated demobilization process, with the purpose of allowing its leaders and soldiers, through a political amnesty, to return to employment and "business as usual." The government accepted this and invited the OAS (Organization of American States) to monitor and verify the demobilization. Although it began in 2004, a legal framework for this process was not established until 2005 through Law 975. This law was highly controversial and, as we shall see, is widely debated inside and outside Colombia.

Law 975

In an attempt to regulate the legal dimensions of the demobilization of soldiers in the paramilitary groups, the Colombian congress issued Law 975 in 2005, which they intended to serve as the legal framework for paramilitary, as well as leftist guerilla groups, if and when they were prepared to enter into peace negotiations with the Colombian government. The law tries to identify a balancing point between the social and political needs for an end to violence, on the one hand, and the protection of victims' rights and a guarantee of non-repetition, on the other. Law 975 was approved by the Congress of Colombia and thereafter revised—and sharpened—by the Colombian Constitutional Court, which oversees the constitutionality of laws. Although often described as a "law of impunity," largely due to the inefficiency of the Colombian judicial system, the law itself cannot be described as one of outright impunity. It clearly offers leniency in the penalties for a number of crimes committed by the groups concerned during their period of combat. Depending on the nature and combinations of the crimes, Law 975—after being revised by the Constitutional Court—proscribes a minimum penalty of five years, and a maximum of eight, for those that demobilize, cooperate with the court, and in other ways comply with the demands of the law. This is the balancing point identified by the Constitutional Court. While accepting the principle of transitional justice in Colombia as part of a peace process, the Court set a minimum justice threshold of five years, but at the same time put an upper limit on accumulated penalties.

In 2008 all significant paramilitary leaders were extradited to the United States, wanted for their narcotic trafficking. This action closed the internal Colombian legal procedure over the AUC leaders and their political and narcotic trafficking involvement. For the foreseeable future it also closed the possibility of a peace process involving the paramilitary leaders in the country. Thus, the much-debated Law 975 did not come to be seriously tested.

Law 975 illustrates the dilemma of protecting human rights, on the one hand, and on the other hand securing an end to direct violence and thereby establishing negative peace, i.e., law and order after armed violence. While there are many and special circumstances in the case of the paramilitary groups of Colombia, the dilemma is the same as in other countries—such as Bosnia-Herzegovina—where every attempt to put an end to the massacres, murders and extra-judicial killings is pursued as a defense of fundamental human rights.

Livelihood and Confidence Issues

As a way of summarizing some critical points in each case presented here, one can construct the following image based on livelihood and confidence issues for Colombia.

FIGURE 5: Reinforcing Issues in the Colombian Situation

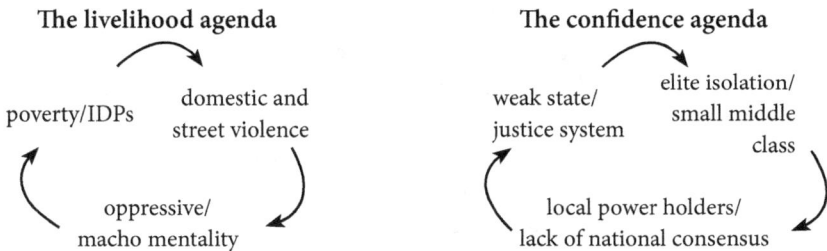

The livelihood agenda

poverty/IDPs   domestic and street violence

oppressive/ macho mentality

The confidence agenda

weak state/ justice system   elite isolation/ small middle class

local power holders/ lack of national consensus

Colombia has one of the largest populations of internally displaced people (IDP). At the same time, the country is seriously asymmetric in terms of wealth distribution—the middle class is small, and power is concentrated in the hands of the few, the elite. The *livelihood* agenda is dominated by abject poverty, which strikes sporadically and in various parts of the country. For obvious reasons—in particular among young persons—this leads to survival techniques other than work: street violence, theft, and concomitant actions rooted in a of lack self-confidence which seeks compensation in a macho lifestyle.

Domestic violence is common and sometimes increasing in the wake of reduced violence between armed groups and the government. Returning soldiers do not always become peaceful at home—rather the opposite. The circle of survival-based violence seems unbroken. An effective state could break from this if it not were for its own weakness, which thus creates a serious *confidence* problem. The state's inability to deal with local power holders and the lack of a sizeable middle class that could take a mediating role between the extremes, which are very far apart in the Colombian society, results in a very polarized and fragmented society. As the power balance changes between the government, its army, and local power holders, the negative peace—law and order—

comes and goes in cities and regions. The election of a new president, Juan Manuel Santos, in 2010 will not change this fundamental feature of the Colombian society.

From the Horizon of the NGOs

It is against this historic situation that a group of NGOs participated in a seminar in Colombia in 2007, discussing the overlapping agendas of Human Rights and Peace-Building in a Colombian context.[3] Colombia is presently in a situation where many ask the question: "Which principle should take prevalence in a peace process—justice or peace?" This issue results in lively discussion in light of the various attempts to formulate conditions for a peace between the government and various groups in the country. Some human rights organizations would argue that the principle of peace has to be subordinated to the principle of justice. Some peace organizations, but also politicians, would argue the opposite, claiming that as long as the rebels or the ("old" or "new") paramilitaries have some power there will never be even a minimum of peace (negative peace) if justice should be applied first. What some consensus-building organizations would argue is that justice needs be organized in a way that it is fulfilled as time goes by, but at the same time is not blocking the way towards peace. That is to say, there should first be the establishment of a negative peace and later on the realization of a positive peace.

Another approach taken in the Colombian debate has been that there are a number of components in concepts of justice and peace— such as truth—that are necessary for the realization of both peace and justice. Therefore one should, as a method, utilize truth as a *bridging concept* to start the peace process by relating truth, peace, and justice to each other in a constructive way instead of positioning them against each other. In the same way, the need for reparation for victims is part of a societal compensation and repayment for its failure to protect human rights, according to this view. It should not necessarily be the perpetrator on an individual level that "pays back" the victims; the perpetrator may not even be alive, or for other reasons is unable to redress the injuries committed. In the end it becomes the responsibility of the state to

3. The participating organizations were Centro de Investigación y Educación Popular (CINEP), Asamblea Permanente de la Sociedad Civil para la Paz (APSCP), and Alianza de Organizaciones Sociales y Afines (Alianza). For a collection of papers from the seminar in Colombia 2007, see *Derechos Humanos*.

guarantee that reparations are made in an appropriate way. Thus, there are some aspects of justice that can be realized without really threatening the dilemma of peace and justice. Perhaps there is not really—at least not necessarily and always—a dilemma. Maybe the debate has been too general and too ingrained with generalizations and prejudices among those debating so that a sober understanding of what is actually possible has not been visible until the issues are really put at loggerheads against each other.

It is a commonly held position among Colombian NGOs that it is easy to forget the responsibility of the state in the discussion about human rights and peace-building. While some express an understanding of the need for transitional justice in a period of return to peace and normality—a position also taken by the Constitutional Court of Colombia—there is no reason, at the same time, to accept the flaws and deficiencies of the judiciary, which include lackluster police investigations, failures to prosecute, and an inappropriate jail system. Such weaknesses of the state, it is argued, create a high risk of a *de facto* impunity, even if the laws do not provide for it. This situation creates a triangle of power relations in the transitional process. Instead of balancing between the needs to induce groups to stop war and violence, on the one hand, and enforcing the demands of the law, on the other hand, we have a third factor to consider in the weakness of the state to implement whatever legal requirement there is.

A second approach to the situation in Colombia, which has relevance for many other situations as well, is the tendency to "blame all problems on the war." Injustices entrenched in cultural patterns and habits, long-term developments towards increased differences between groups and regions, and the failure of politicians to act in due time against street violence can all be attributed to the consequences of an ongoing internal armed conflict. This double role of an armed conflict—to be used as an explanation of unsolved problems and at the same time as the origin of existing problems—is a major challenge to NGOs and organizations that try to deal with specific issues of development and social justice in Colombia, as well as in other countries with similar situations. This situation also points, more or less directly, towards the fact that certain social groups have a lot to gain from ongoing conflict. Not only the security establishment, but also political groups and politicians with an agenda based on the existence of an armed conflict, have more to gain from the continuation of violence than from addressing the existence of grave injustices.

To make just one conclusion from meeting with Colombian NGOs, many would argue that the issue should be more about how human rights, in all their width and depth, can be protected in a durable way in the long run, rather than if they can be protected to a full extent under a critical moment of a transitional process on national level. To find a balancing point between peace and justice, when neither of them can be fully realized, is, according to this view, the real challenge.

DEMOCRATIC REPUBLIC OF CONGO

The Democratic Republic of the Congo (DRC), being the third largest country in Africa, covers a considerable area of central Africa. Former names of the country, like the Congo Free State and Belgian Congo, imply a long colonial history before the independence attained in 1960. At the beginning of the twentieth century King Leopold II of Belgium presided over a political system in Congo in which slave labor caused the death of approximately ten million people.[4] Independence was followed by five years of unrest and instability before Mobutu Sese Seko took over the country in 1971 and renamed it Zaïre. Thirty years of dictatorship characterized by neglect, corruption, a cult of personality, political repression, and severe violations of human rights followed.

In the DRC 250 ethnic groups have been identified and named, and there are several hundred local languages and dialects spoken. The combination of enormous distances, challenging terrain, special climate, financial weakness, and violent conflicts has made transportation severely difficult and rivers, which offer traditional ways of transport, remain crucial. One aspect of this situation is the difficulty of a central government to control and be present in every region and village.

In the human development index the Democratic Republic of Congo is ranked 168th of 177 countries.[5] GDP per capita for 2005 was $123 U.S., which can be compared with $39,637 U.S. for Sweden. While the DRC may be considered to be one of the poorest countries in the world, it is at the same time a resource-rich country. The DRC has attractive natural resources, especially in the eastern part of the country. Being

---

4. Hochschild, *King Leopold's Ghost*, 225–34.
5. *Human Development Report 2007/2008*, 280.

the world's largest producer of cobalt and a significant producer of copper, industrial diamonds, tantalum, and tin have also caused exploitation and violent conflicts.[6]

The war and genocide in Rwanda in 1996 spread into neighboring Congo through fleeing refugees and militias. When opposition groups and local warlords became involved, the country was exposed to a devastating war sometimes named the "African World War," since it involved not only different local militias and rebel groups but also several foreign armies. President Mobutu fled Zaïre, and Laurent-Désiré Kabila with his army entered into Kinshasa with Kabila ending up as the president in May 1997. In 1998 Jean-Pierre Bemba and his Mouvement pour la Liberation du Congo, backed by Rwandan and Ugandan troops, attacked the government supported by Angola, Zimbabwe, and Namibia in 1998. The conflict escalated and for a time became the deadliest conflict since the Second World War. At least 5.4 million Congolese were killed.

The Lusaka Ceasefire Agreement was signed in July 1999 between the DRC and five other regional states. In an effort to maintain a liaison with the parties, the UN Security Council set up a UN peace-keeping operation, MONUC, in November 1999 to facilitate the implementation of the Lusaka Accord. When Kabila was assassinated in 2001 he was succeeded by his son Joseph Kabila. A peace deal involving Joseph Kabila, Rwanda, and Burundi was signed in February 2001 and MONUC arrived in April. But clashes in the east of the DRC continued between ethnic groups and between militias/rebels and the regular army, even with a foreign military presence in the area. It became obvious that the violent military activities were focused on gaining control of the natural resources.

In a serious attempt to stop the civil war in the eastern parts of Congo, the Pretoria Agreement was signed in July 2002, an agreement that included the withdrawal of Rwandan troops from the DRC and the dismantling of the ex-Rwandan and Interahamwe militia. Some months later, an overriding agreement was signed in December 2002 for a transitional period, with Kabila as president and a power-sharing arrangement involving rebel groups in the government until elections could be held twenty-four months later. The next step was taken in March 2003 when a more detailed agreement on transitional arrangements, dealing with the establishment of an integrated national army, was signed. This agree-

6. See Custers and Nordbrand, *Risky Business*.

ment enabled a transitional government. Besides the government, the agreement was signed by RCD-ML (Rassemblement Congolais pour la Démocrati Mouvement de Libération du Congo), RCD (Rassemblement Congolais pour la Démocratie), MLC (Mouvement de Libération du Congo), RCD-N (Rassemblement Congolais pour la Démocratie/ National), and representatives from the Maï-Maï movement, as well as by thirty persons from the political opposition and twenty-seven individuals representing the civil society. One major group, however, refused to sign: the UPC (Union des Patriotes Congolais).

The scheduled elections were postponed several times before parliamentary and presidential elections were finally held in October 2006. These were the first multiparty free elections in forty years in the DRC, something that gave some hope for the future.

But still there are severe problems in the east with violent clashes and grave violations against the human rights. Reports from the DRC talk about serious human rights abuses and renewed tensions in the east of the country. The security situation has improved but remains fragile and there is an ongoing displacement of the civilian population.

Livelihood and Confidence Issues

As a way of summarizing some critical points concerning the livelihood and confidence agendas in the case presented here, one can construct the following image for at least the eastern part of the DRC.

FIGURE 6: Reinforcing Issues in the Congolese (DRC) Situation

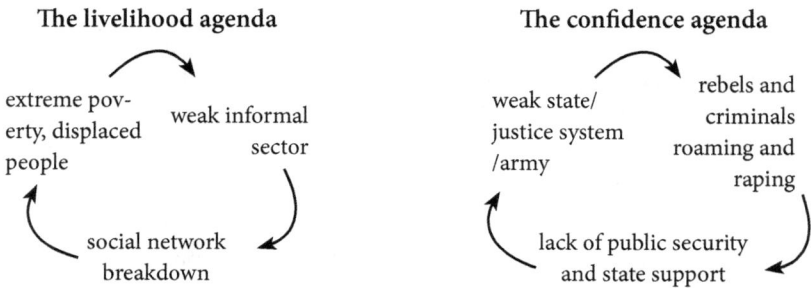

The livelihood agenda

extreme poverty, displaced people → weak informal sector → social network breakdown →

The confidence agenda

weak state/ justice system /army → rebels and criminals roaming and raping → lack of public security and state support →

The Livelihood Agenda drawn here is one way of representing the private sectors of the civil society in the eastern part of the Democratic Republic of Congo. The lack of security for personal life, due in large part to the enormous numbers of people killed and women raped, has left people in extreme poverty. A big number of internally displaced people adds to that situation. The formal sector is almost non-existent and the informal sector weak. With families splintered and villages uprooted the traditional social networks based on family and tribal belonging are facing a breakdown. The Confidence Agenda follows closely the same pattern. The state is trying to get a grip on the countryside but is very weak both in providing protection and granting justice. Rebels, military groups, and criminal gangs—some with aspirations to control natural resources for foreign use—are the counterparts struggling with the state to get power. The situation is characterized by a lack of public security and a lack of civil society support.

From the Horizon of the NGOs

Organizations and institutions in the Bukavu region in the eastern part of the DRC, as well as in the capital Kinshasa, have in common that they are working, in one or another way, with human rights and/or peace-building activities.[7] Their strategies include collecting data, lobbying, and running seminars and educational programs in a range of subjects including alphabetization, democratization, gender, conflict resolution, and human rights. In general, the organizations are focusing on singular issues, like women's issues, children, peasants, illegal imprisonment and impunity, education, or radio broadcasting. Health is also an important subject, including fighting HIV, malaria, and other diseases. Some of the organizations are umbrella organizations representing an extensive number of local and national bodies, while other are locally based such as those working in Kabare territory. Several of the organizations deal with monitoring of human rights violations in grassroots communities

7. Action pour le Développement et la Paix Endogènes ADEPAE, Association des Femme des Medias du Sud-Kivu, Action Sociale pour la Femme et l'Enfant Defavourise (ASFED), Action Sociale et d'Organisation Paysanne (ASOP), Groupe Jeremieh, Les Amies de Nelson Mandela pour la Défense des Droites Humains, Radio Maendeleo Reseau des Femme pour la defence des Droite et la Paix (RFDP), RODHERIC, Université Protestante au Congo, Voi de sans voi, National Network of Congolese HR and COJESKI. The authors met with these organizations in 2008.

in both the provinces and Kinshasa. This may be done through field visits or organizing seminars.

As an example, a concrete project aims at countering violence among young people in lower Congo by training them in non-violence and democracy. Another project is training women, who have been victims of violations in South-Kivu, to understand the conflict, the agents, and how to get involved as actors. They are being encouraged to intervene in different decision-making levels in order to solve the conflict, point out ongoing violations against women, and report to local authorities and the government. A third project aims at promoting human rights and specifically women rights through the media.

Peace and Human Rights

In their work, these organizations frequently seem to use both the concept of peace and the concept of human rights. There are different levels of these concepts involved, partly because the eastern part of the country is in a post-war situation, but frequently military activities and fighting take place between different militant groups and the Congolese army. Consequently, one way of imagining the concept of peace will indicate a situation with an absence of war and foreign influence, while another might depict a situation with no more groups or armies raping, sexual harassing, looting, etc. Another way of expressing peace will concentrate much more on the local situation in a village or a city. Then peace will more or less correspond to coexistence and harmony. This may be expressed as "everybody must live in harmony and peace," "we need to settle problems in harmony and in a peaceful way," or that it is important for the population to "maintain harmony among themselves." Traditional values like unity, solidarity, community work, and the interest of the whole community are then supporting peace.

Sometimes peace and human rights go hand in hand in representing the basic conditions for a decent living. The discussion concerning what is most important in a local village may run along this line of thought:

> The most important issue is peace. The people in the village need security, something to eat, water, transportation and they need development. That is human rights and people will name it human rights.

In this way human rights and peace will indicate a vision for a post-war situation. Peace is not only absence of war but the presence of moral, social, economic, and environmental preconditions for human beings to take part in a good life. There may be a difference between people in cities and in the countryside. Having in mind that all human rights are indivisible and indispensable, there can be priorities in the local situation. The aspirations of middle-class townspeople can be seen focusing on civil and political rights while people in villages aspire for social and economic rights reflecting the basic need for survival.

Even if human rights and peace can be looked upon as two sides of the same coin there are also possibilities to see peace following in the steps of human rights. This can be expressed through statements like: "put all human rights violations on the table since there is a need to address them on the way to get peace"; "human rights violations might be the key to why people do not have peace"; and "when people know their rights that will help them to live in peace in their communities." The focus is then on the need to first implement human rights for the people.

The basic need and top priority of the people in the countryside is to fight starvation, to cultivate crops and carry out husbandry, and therefore these need to be part of development. Going into detail, this may include making their own compost, protecting the soil to ensure it is fertile, awareness of the dangers of erosion, farming suitable crops, breeding small animals such as hens and goats, ensuring fish spawn in local waters, and keeping bees for honey. The link between poverty and the absence of peace is strong. Human rights are believed to include addressing problems with access to land, provision of food, poverty, and sanitation. Preconditions for peace are connected with rights in relation to land, possibilities for work, education, and health. The fulfillment of rights to basic living conditions is looked upon as a peaceful solution after conflict.

Security, Power, and Human Rights Violations

The organizations we met hold the position that in the African context human rights are to this point significantly neglected. In many instances women have no right to speech and are not involved in men's decision-making processes. Human rights are violated in the DRC because people lack knowledge about them. There is also weakness of the institutions established to protect human rights, and those who are asked to promote human rights lack knowledge. To this should be added that there is a culture of impunity.

With an almost united voice, NGOs in the east of the DRC call for a system where the power is in the hands of the people. Usually they are not looking for the state to take care of them. Rather, it is the village as a community that matters. What they basically ask for is to get rid of a system that performs, and even cultivates, violations against human rights. It is a question of identifying and naming power structures and mechanisms of control that prevent human rights implementation and the fulfillment of peace. What people in that situation seem to ask for is to get rid of structures hindering basic security.

There are still several armed groups promulgating war upon the people and sometimes they resemble criminal gangs rather than rebel groups. A complicating factor is that different segments of the population have ethnic and tribal identities upon which sympathies for either the government or different militant groups and militias, who claim they are protecting their own people, are based. Voices in the east are also convinced there are, at least occasionally, foreign troops on the ground or foreign support for local militias. Until those militias are demobilized and the regions are under the control of the national army, basic security will be lacking and even in the post-conflict situation the war may erupt again at any moment.

Many foreign companies working with mines, for example, create a situation where it has become a problem to fulfill and respect human rights. The claim is that the war in Congo is a war about natural resources and that different companies are stealing them. The companies are accused of misusing the local population and not taking into account the needs of local people.

The main violators of the human rights are the police, soldiers in the regular army, governmental administrators, judges, etc. The situation is worst in the countryside. The problem is that the officials are not necessary locals but have been sent to a specific area on behalf of the authorities. Soldiers and police are especially pointed out for being culprits with the reason being that they have extremely poor salaries. Voices from the east are claiming: "A police officer can do and take anything he want"; "people are killed in their homes and on the road, and they are robbed"; "the police have arms and they are hungry and come to the people and commit crimes"; and "those not respecting human rights are those who should protect human rights." In relation to this, the corruption is endemic in the police force and other local authorities, with money being sent upward in the hierarchy.

What is expressed in terms of power and control is a lack of confidence in the political system by ordinary people, along with a failure of politicians to establish institutions and mechanisms granting the people basic security under the umbrella of the authorities. As long as basic security is not granted human rights will continue to be violated and there will be no peace.

Sexual Harassment, the Law, and Traditional Customs

The Democratic Republic of Congo ratified the Rome Statutes in 2002 and since then rape and sexual violence are considered crimes. The new law states that anyone committing a sexual crime must be punished and forbids the traditional resolution through "peaceful agreements." Yet severe crimes involving sexual violence are still being committed: "women are taken into the forest by armed troops" and "our area is an area where soldiers go and they kidnap and sexually assault our daughters, sisters, etc." Women have been brutality raped and exposed to extreme sexual violence by members of armed groups or criminal gangs, but also by soldiers in the army, police officers, and even fellow villagers. The impact on the family is tragic, with traumatized people and severe health problems including the spread of HIV. Stigmatized for life, the women are often rejected by their husbands and expelled from their families, villages, and even their local churches. Still people look for justice.

Of course, what is done by rebel groups is more or less out of the control of a government who is at war with those groups. But in other cases, according to the law, what they do should be filed and dealt with in the legal system. However, at least in the east of the DRC, very few trust the court system. A great number of seemingly fair reasons are given for this. The court system is not developed in such a way that it covers the entire country. This means a lot of people, not least those living in the countryside and in the east, will have a long journey to reach a court, more or less making it unreachable. Due to low salaries there is a lack of manpower in the existing courts, and to this should be added the prominent issue of corruption. Both costly travels and costly bribes, in combination with the poverty of many villagers, inhibit their access to power. The modern law is written in a language usually not understood in the countryside where numerous local languages are spoken.

Making peaceful agreements "under the mango tree" is a traditional method of "peaceful reconciliation" or "peaceful conflict resolution." Basically there are three steps involved in these processes:

1. getting people to talk to each other;

2. settling the conflict among themselves;

3. avoidance of one party being a winner and the other a loser.

When discussing peaceful agreements, one of the organizations said:

> There is no fine to pay with friendly settlement. The only fine is just to repair the damages. The parts in conflict make reconciliation in a ceremony and at the end they are friends and gain confidence. People share a glass of wine and everyone is satisfied. In the modern way you make a case and penalties imposed on the loser.

The aim is to strengthen the social cohesion in the village, and several of the NGOs talk about peace coming out of these agreements, while others imply there are problems. In different local settings there are different hierarchies of compensation. As an example, when the Bukavu people pursue a peaceful agreement in a case where a woman is raped, the rapist is asked to give a goat (scapegoat) as compensation. For other crimes the parties involved share a glass of wine. In a situation where a house is burned down, the individual responsible for starting the fire has to participate in the rebuilding project. A peaceful agreement is completed between the men involved in the incident, usually the perpetrator and the husband, father or brother. They agree upon a solution that may involve compensation with the aim of keeping harmony and peace in the village. But still, the female victim remains a victim who is often rejected and isolated. Some agree this is a huge dilemma and that problems involving violence are not satisfactorily resolved for the victim, especially when sexual crimes are involved.

Committing War-Crimes—Getting Amnesty

Since 2003 the DRC has been undergoing a post-conflict reconstruction. A level of peace has been achieved with a demilitarization process, withdrawal of foreign troops, and elections. Still, in the eastern part of the country, mainly North and South Kivu, violence on the local level continues. Factionalized groups such as the Maï-Maï as well as renegade soldiers from the regular Congolese army are acting with violence in the area, not least based on ethnic affiliations or as some have called it, "the manipulation of ethnicity."

The demilitarization of combatants is under way, but what is to be done with the responsible leaders? In many cases, they have been responsible for committing acts possible to describe, with reference to the Rome Statute, as "the most serious crimes," such as crimes against humanity and war crimes. Can it be justified to involve them in the peace process and negotiations? Should they be free to walk around in the area after an amnesty or is there a need to send them to the International Criminal Court? Can people believe in human rights, justice, and peace if the leaders are not prosecuted?

GUATEMALA

Guatemala is one of the countries in Central America that geographically binds together North and South America. Although a small country (measuring about 100,000 sq km) it drew international media attention over several decades for its devastating internal conflict. It lasted from 1962 to 1996[8] and included serious and systematic violations of human rights on a scale that can be identified as crimes against humanity and other serious violations. All actors were rightfully accused of such acts: the military, the police, and numerous private armies, as well as the guerilla groups involved.

Many countries in the Latin America share the historic and political fate of Guatemala—independence during the first part of the nineteenth century, and a long period of military and/or autocratic regimes without any real conditions for a democratic development, internal wars, and, in the twentieth century, leftist guerilla opposition groups and liberation armies in armed confrontations with governments as well as private armies and paramilitaries. After the Second World War, the East-West division of the Cold war polarized these conflicts. In Latin America, the United States—with its relative proximity to the region—played a particularly important role as a supporter of rightist governments—

---

8. Obviously the conflict issues are very old and structurally rooted. The violent phase of the most recent and violent period of conflict began in 1962.

democratic or not. The Soviet Union, on its side, and with strong links with Cuba, supported the leftist movements in the region, whether as fighting guerilla groups or in government.

It was not until the Cold War had ended that the peace process in Guatemala, as in many of its neighboring countries, could make real progress, but it should be recognized that some significant steps were taken before that as well. Agreements could, for instance, be reached through efforts from regional political leaders in the 1980s (the Contadora Group 1983–1985). One such important agreement was the Esquipulas II agreement of 1987. Particularly important for this was President of Costa Rica and Nobel Peace Prize Laureate, Oscar Arias.

The long conflict period in Guatemala resulted in the death or disappearance of at least 200,000, over a million refugees—mostly to Mexico—and a significant number of internally displaced people (IDP). Today the figure of IDPs is disputed. While UNHCR claims there are no IDPs, national NGOs monitoring the situation claim the figure to be several hundred thousand.[9] The main parties in the conflict for a long period were the leftist guerilla umbrella organization URNG (Guatemalan National Revolutionary Unit), which was created in 1982, and the various military, democratic, and/or civilian governments from that time. While the conflict was initially focused on land reform issues—with liberal sectors of the Guatemalan society trying to create a more just distribution of land—this reform process was abruptly broken by private landlords supported by the military and international/multinational companies who saw all their holdings being put at risk through such a policy. As the conflict unfolded, issues of identity (a majority of the Guatemalan population is of Mayan descent), democratic influence, workers' rights, and economic justice became equally important parts of the conflict agenda.

The peace process, once it started, took several years and sought to incorporate all the major issues. Major contributing agreements were, for instance, the global accord on human rights in March 1994, the accord on the resettlement of the internally displaced people in June 1994, the accord on the establishment of a commission for historical clarification ("truth commission") on past human rights abuses in June 1994,

---

9. Internal Displacement Monitoring Centre, "Guatemala: Global IDP Figures," http://www.internal-displacement.org/idmc/website/countries.nsf/(httpEnvelopes)/EE 4DEA6CC40B5692802570B8005A7316?OpenDocument.

and an accord on the rights and identities of indigenous peoples signed in March 1995.

In the negotiations, not only the government, the guerilla leadership, and the UN participated, but also The Group of Friends (Colombia, Mexico, Norway, Spain, the United States and Venezuela), the Catholic Church, the media, and the Civil Society Assembly (ASC), which had the role of presenting a document as a starting point for the negotiations over each topic. The role of civil society organizations—in their various forms—in this process was critical and led to direct and indirect effects in Guatemalan society that would not otherwise have been seen, such as capacity-building, political awareness, and identity formation.

In the peace process the URNG finally turned itself into a civil political party. The final agreement was signed in 1996 under the auspices of the United Nations, and a new administration, under President Arzú, was inaugurated in Guatemala in January 1996.

It is not an exaggeration to claim that Guatemala, in the years after the peace agreement, lacked both institutional capacity and political will to implement the visions, concrete proposals, and agreed principles of the many accords included in the peace process. It seems that the longing for an end to more than four decades of civil war made the signing of an agreement more important than securing its successful implementation. This is understandable and not a unique experience to Guatemala. At the same time it should be remembered that the peace process in Guatemala was the most comprehensive in Latin America up until that time. It involved all major sectors of the society and it gave a central and critical role to the civil society in the process. Therefore it had strong legitimacy nationally and internationally. It served as a source of inspiration for similar processes in other countries in the Central American region as well.

Today, civil society organizations in Guatemala, such as churches and NGOs, often indicate a double feeling vis-à-vis the peace process of the 1990s. On the one hand, it was a significant experience that legitimized a major mobilization and leading role of civil society, which could not be as active and competent today without this experience. On the other hand, civil society is dependent on an active state, and even protection from the state, in a country where corruption, private armies, and politics through threats is the order of the day. It may even have been a sort of naïveté to believe that this culture of the power-holding groups should disappear after a peace agreement. Thus, today civil society is challenged physically, politically, and institutionally—maybe on a level never seen before—due to the lack of basic security in Guatemalan society. Extra-judiciary killings, murder, rape, threats, administrative red tape, and outright denial of legal rights are daily experiences of the church, the civil society, and many democratic political groups in Guatemala today.

Memory and truth were keys in the peace process. The Catholic Church of Guatemala published a report in 1998, *Nunca Más* (Never Again), from its project on the recuperation of historical memory. The Commission of Historical Clarification fulfilled its work and presented the report *Guatemala: Memoria del Silencio* in 1999. In different and complementary ways these reports raised and clarified both the horrors of the past and the need for justice in its most basic terms. The reports challenged the fundamentals of the economic and political interests of the Guatemalan elite. Two days after the publication of the Church report, the Archbishop of Guatemala at the time, Msg. Gerardi, was murdered.

If one concept should be used to illustrate Guatemala historically, as a society, it is *exclusion*. Throughout the centuries, a majority of the Guatemalan population—foremost the indigenous groups, but also others—have been systematically exploited and repressed for cultural, economic, and political reasons. The cultural violence that legitimized this repression was and is very strong and it is interesting to remember that the revolt of the 1960s did not actually come from the indigenous groups, but from liberal and leftist-oriented elite groups among the Spanish descendants of Guatemala. Throughout the decades of conflict, the indigenous dimension became stronger and stronger. The mobilization in political terms also led to a mobilization in identity terms for the indigenous groups.[10]

Livelihood and Confidence Issues

In Guatemala the Livelihood and Confidence Agendas can be described in the following way.

---

10. There are over twenty Maya-related indigenous language groups in Guatemala.

FIGURE 7: Reinforcing Issues in the Guatemalan Situation

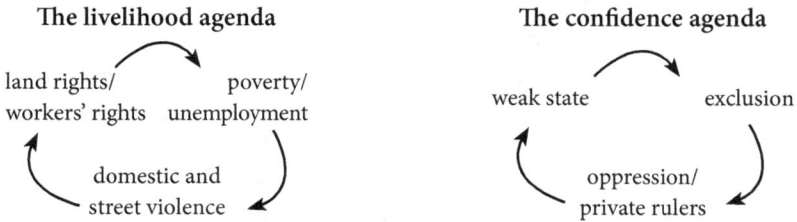

The livelihood agenda   **The confidence agenda**

land rights/   poverty/
workers' rights   unemployment   weak state   exclusion

        domestic and   oppression/
          street violence   private rulers

Already in the 1950s and 1960s the land issue was critical in Guatemala in the sense that it marked the line between inclusion and exclusion in the society, a division with reference to democratic rights, economy, health, education, etc. The land issue was then, as it is today, the critical *livelihood* issue. Land rights and workers' rights were major themes in the long civil war. It was dealt with in one of many processes and agreements in the peace process. Lack of access to, influence on, and ownership of land for agricultural reasons is forcing the young generation into other activities, often in the cities if not internationally. Poverty, an almost unavoidable effect of unemployment, demands ways to maintain both personal self-esteem and survival techniques. Both of them have violent consequences. The violent circle of livelihood is clearly visible in this way. The state, on its part, is struggling to maintain and establish control in order to gain some basic *confidence* among its citizens. This has long been a futile process in Guatemala. Private landholders and international companies have long been ruling through their own agendas and means, which include private armies and the police. Their agendas maintain exclusion, keep the state away, and cement structurally motivated oppression and exclusion into a vicious circle as described above.

From the Horizon of the NGOs

It is not uncommon to hear the expression that "nothing has changed" among members of civil society in Guatemala today. This statement refers to the violence and the economic and political structures compared to the past (1960s–1990s). The issues that are on the table include the lack of fundamental rights, the absent state, impunity, etc. At the same time this is not to say that there are no positive developments on the whole in Guatemalan society after the peace agreement, rather the point is that if the violence of the past was often shrouded in political motives it is today dressed in elite interests, the need for economic control, and for silencing critics through killings and repression. Generally speaking, the level of street violence is higher today than during wartime.

For the state it is important to see the difference between criminality and political violence in order to undertake proper action to deal with it, but for the victims this is a secondary matter: it makes little or no difference what the motives of the perpetrator are when violence strikes. As part of a movement for social change, social responsibility, and peace-building, the civil society of Guatemala lives with both these experiences. It is sometimes a victim of direct violence against its leaders and members, and at the same time the organization has taken on the challenge to analyze and act against the same violence—in a non-violent way—for the improvement of the life conditions of those that need it most.

Human rights and peace-building go hand-in-hand in Guatemala according to many NGOs who talk about their intention to build peace but see human rights violated all the time. "They say we are in a post-conflict situation—the peace agreement is over 10 years now—but at the same time, the violence don't allow us to build peace," as one seminar participant in Guatemala described the situation.[11] What does this mean for NGOs today and their way of dealing with peace and justice? In a seminar in 2007 a number of Guatemalan organizations discussed this and other matters.[12]

Combining Rights and Peace

The struggle for rights, such as the right to land, is at the same time a struggle for dignity, freedom, and therefore peace in the true sense of the word, according to a farmer's organization in Guatemala. The struggle for a minimum salary is both symbolic and a real-life concern. In this way, the wide and comprehensive understanding of peace, as well as the

11. For a collection of papers from the seminar in Guatemala 2007, see *Derechos Humanos*.

12. These organizations were: La Facultad Latinomérica de Ciencias Sociales (FLACSO), Coordinadora Nacional de Organizaciones Campesinos (CNOC), Centro de Reportes Informativos sobre Guatemala (CERIGUA), Consejo de Instituciones de Desarollo (COINDE), Centro Pluricultural para la Democracia "Kemb' al Tinimi" (CPD), La Fundación Myrna Mack (FMM), La Asociación Promujer (Promujer), Oficina de Derechos Humanos del Arzobispado de Guatemala, and FUNDAR—Guatemala.

full realization of human rights, is an idea present in the very specific and seemingly limited struggle for even the slightest, minimum recognition of human dignity and justice.

An issue recognized in the peace process of the 1990s as critical for long-term peace in Guatemala is the land issue. It has many dimensions, from the right to hold land, to the glaring misuse or non-use of land, to the right to defend existing rights to land against economically stronger interests. This issue includes questions of legal rights, of social/working conditions (minimum salaries for instance), and other human rights. In addition—as in many other cases—the weakness of the state to enforce even existing legal requirements makes the social discrimination and exclusion clear to anyone interested in observing it.

For an NGO working on the rights of *campesinos* and rural workers, the peace envisioned in the 1996 peace agreement cannot be realized without a clear development that must begin with equality before the law, respect for at least minimum conditions (such as salaries) and a respected participation in political processes. The peace agreement only represents a formal breaking point, a platform for action, but not the necessary action itself. As noted above, violence continues in Guatemala—in direct and indirect forms. The "peace" is limited to the formal political level: for the working majority life is as hard as ever. The difference is that there is a civil society force towards change. It seems as if all forms of change towards peace have to be rooted in the people, on the level of NGOs and local communities. Maybe that's also why violence is so strong in those communities: the conflict goes on, but in different forms.

For this reason, Guatemala deals with the trauma of the past on the national level and at the same time lives with ongoing trauma on the local level. Reconciliation about the past is perhaps impossible, while violations continue today on the local level. There is not even a limited, negative peace when violence continues. To get it stopped requires both resistance and peace-building to show alternatives: a challenge that the peace agreement never succeeded to make real but now relies on the churches and other NGOs of Guatemala.

One of the conditions upholding the structures of impunity, the rejection of legal requirements, and corruption is the lack of public information about such events and conditions. The killing of journalists or forced silencing through threats and intimidations are effective methods for making information harmless. For any information-providing organization in a country such as Guatemala, the reliance on widely accepted principles for the society are the first and maybe most fundamental defense against such acts. If enough people believe in the need for accurate information, it will be more and more costly to threaten the dissemination of news and information.

Besides the violence in the public sphere, there is in many countries in Latin America, including Guatemala, a severe and entrenched practice of violence against women—in the family and in the private sphere in general. Although sexual and other physical violence are the most troubling forms, the [culturally legitimized] views on the lack of need for schooling and higher education, inheritance, and independent life conditions also converge into strong institutional mechanisms of oppression and curtailed life conditions. It is a well-known fact that civil wars, which normally involve more men than women, result in increased levels of domestic violence—if the soldiers survive in the first place. In addition, a male-dominated *macho* culture should, in the Guatemalan case, be added as contributing to historical and strongly entrenched factors for this.

The Guatemalan experience of historic exclusion, repression, and armed resistance followed by a comprehensive but ineffective peace process created a number of critical issues and problems for the international community. Some of them belong to the theme of this study.

PALESTINE

The sixtieth anniversary of the *Universal Declaration of Human Rights* and the commemoration of sixty years since the adoption of the *Convention on the Prevention and Punishment of the Crime of Genocide* were both held in 2008. These memorial events also coincided with the celebration of sixty years since the establishment of the State of Israel.

The UN General Assembly approved a partition plan in 1947 with the intention of dividing the then British Mandate of Palestine into an Arab state and a Jewish state. This never came into reality when Israel proclaimed itself an independent state in 1948, which was followed by an attack from the neighboring Arab states. The outcome of the war may be seen from the retrospective naming of the war. For the State of Israel it is the War of Independence and for the Palestinians it is the Naqbah, the "great catastrophe."

The areas of the planned Palestinian (Arab) state became partly incorporated into the State of Israel, partly under Jordanian rule (the West Bank), and partly under Egypt (the Gaza Strip). A major geopolitical change took place in 1967 with the Six Day War when Israel occupied the West Bank, the Gaza Strip, and parts of the Syrian Golan Heights. In the following peace process Sinai was handed back to Egypt in 1979. From this date two developments may be seen throughout the years. The first involves a step-by step take over by Israel of the occupied territories through a major settlement policy; control of land, water, and natural resources; and a transfer of its own population into the occupied territories, as well as restrictions on the development of Palestinian areas and restrictions of the movement of the Palestinians (inside as well as in and out of Palestinian areas). The second may be described through military activities from the Israeli side aiming at ruling, controlling, and undertaking security measures, and from the Palestinian side aiming at ending the occupation and establishing an independent Palestinian state.

From the Israeli side, this includes unilateral annexation of East Jerusalem and the areas of the West Bank and the Golan Heights into Israel and a step-by-step establishing of "facts on the ground" through more settlements, new bypass roads (around Palestinian villages), and the building of a wall (security barrier) mainly on occupied Palestinian land. From the Palestinian side the same period may be characterized by shrinking possibilities for a normal life and livelihood as well as for political aspirations of independence or self-determination. The Palestinian protests in this period after the Six Day War have culminated in two uprisings (Intifadas) followed—through the Oslo process in the 1990s—by the establishment of a Palestinian local political structure. The situation following the latest elections in the West Bank and Gaza—the outcome of which was rejected internationally—has turned into one of internal Palestinian political and violent military activities, not the least between the Palestinian National Authority and the Hamas movement.

Agreements, Reconciliation, and Human Rights

With certain regularity over the years and through international pressure and mediation, peace initiatives and even agreements have been put in place. But so far most of these initiatives have either failed as a whole or resulted in outcomes short of the broadly supported view of a realistic solution to the conflict between Israel and Palestine—a two-state solution.

As Jaana Rokka shows in a study for this project,[13] almost every peace initiative in the modern Middle East conflict situation includes preconditions for peaceful coexistence, confidence, and support for a democratic culture with justice, truth, healing, and compensation. Since the main issue in the conflict never has come close to a settlement, in combination with a general suspicion between the parties, these mechanisms have not been activated.

In an article the General Director of the Palestinian NGO Al-Haq, Shawan Jabarin, discusses this situation.[14] Failures can, according to him, be ascribed to continuing disregard and an ongoing indifference to human rights. Each political agreement needs to address the reality on the ground. Concerning the West Bank this refers to the occupation as "a major cause for the continuing degradation and infringement of human rights."[15]

> [w]e continue to ignore international law and human rights, and, as a result, the status quo, the cycle of violence and suffering will perpetuate. We will reach political agreements on paper but no genuine, just or lasting peace, and no side will really gain.[16]

Without positive changes, and at the same time continuing systematic violations of human rights, the Palestinian public loses hope. It seems, as a conclusion, that an end of the occupation is a necessary prerequisite for finding a sustainable solution for the future.

Livelihood and Confidence Issues

In the Palestinian territories there is a complex web of livelihood and confidence issues. In a way they all relate to each other through the strong impact in the areas from Israeli presence (the occupation) and international involvement.

13. Rokka, *Att konfronteras.*

14. The article is based on Al-Haq's experience of working in the field for thirty years. See Jabarin, *Peace and Human Rights.*

15. Jabarin, *Peace and Human Rights*, 4.

16. Ibid., 6.

FIGURE 8: Reinforcing Issues in the Palestinian Situation

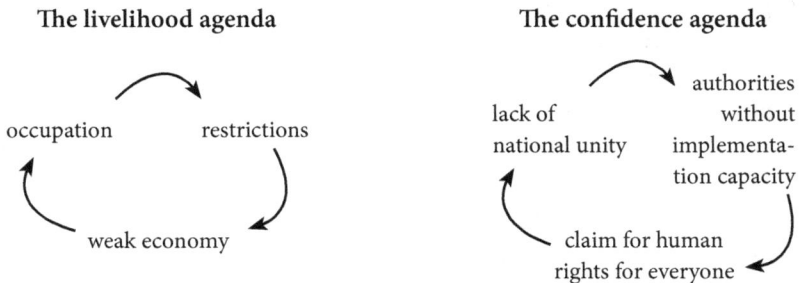

The livelihood agenda   **The confidence agenda**

occupation   restrictions

weak economy

authorities
lack of   without
national unity   implementation capacity

claim for human
rights for everyone

The situation for Palestine is today closely linked to the State of Israel, which is clearly seen in the Livelihood agenda. The occupation is, for most of the people in the Palestinian territories, a lifelong experience. Daily life is limited by laws, restrictions, and regulations originating in the occupation where military control, Israeli settlements' taking over land and water, as well as the wall/security barrier is cutting through Palestinian land. This leads to a weaker and weaker Palestinian economy and the hand of the occupation is experienced as harder and harder. The Confidence agenda is today marked by a lack of national unity among the Palestinians. The democratic elections—rejected by the U.S. and Western Europe—have led to a division among the Palestinians that is escalating into military violence. Authorities do exist but the situation gives them few possibilities or financial resources for implementation of the rule of law. Ordinary people, as well as civil society in general, are actively claiming human rights for each and everyone.

From the Horizon of the NGOs

When discussing human rights and peace we are, in this part of the chapter, mainly focusing on the situation in Palestine (the Palestinian Territories, Palestine under occupation, the West Bank and the Gaza Strip) in connection to the Israeli military occupation on one hand, and the Palestinian Authority and other actors on the other. It is not the situation inside the State of Israel that is in focus, even if we are aware about all problems connected to suicide bombings, issues of security, etc. We are also aware of the situation inside Palestine with, due to disagreement, one authority in Palestine/Gaza and another in Palestine/West Bank.

Palestinian NGOs working with human rights issues regularly come back to statements like: "Without respect for human rights there can be no peace." The experience is that activities and efforts made to achieve peace have been without any success and, at least from the Palestinian side, looked upon as failure after failure. The main reason is that the proposed peace has not been considered as a peace with justice. One root cause for the situation is the occupation and a solution regularly put forward is to end the occupation.

Israeli NGOs like B'tselem, in their work, take as a point of departure human rights violations in the Occupied Territories. A primary concern is that the Israeli government's rule over the Occupied Territories must protect the human rights of the residents. The international community, as well as the International Court of Justice, consider the occupation as illegal and therefore demand that the occupation must come to an end. Most Israeli NGOs agree that using International Humanitarian Law and human rights as guiding principles so far has been a failure in setting the situation.

The Palestinian organization Al-Haq, affiliated to the International Commission of Jurists, produce regular field reports after documenting human rights abuses and violations conducted by Israel as an occupying power, as well as abuses committed by the Palestinian National Authority (PNA) and abuses committed by the Hamas authority in the Gaza Strip.[17] The State of Israel is accused of, for example, targeted assassinations and willful killings, harassment and beating by Israeli soldiers, the demolition of houses for punitive reasons, property destruction and/or confiscation, the forcible displacement of people, restrictions on movement, land confiscation and/or destruction, arbitrary arrests, destruction of ministerial buildings, and withholding of PNA tax revenues. The PNA is accused of, for example, arbitrary arrests, vigilantism, torture, and other forms of ill-treatment, and Hamas, finally, is accused of committing extra-judicial killings and executions.

Those Israeli human rights organizations that focus on the human rights situation in the Occupied Territories list numerous violations. In their statistical material the first issue of concern is killings in various forms. This can be Palestinians killed by Israeli security forces or by Israeli civilians, as well as Israeli civilians killed by Palestinians, Israeli security force personnel killed by Palestinians, foreign citizens killed

---

17. *Field Report.*

by Palestinians or by Israeli security forces, and Palestinians killed by Palestinians.

With all these developments in mind we choose here to pick up one concrete and recent example, the Gaza War in 2009.

The 2009 Gaza War[18]

In 2008 a six-month ceasefire between Hamas and Israel ended on December 19 without a solution in reach regarding the isolation of Gaza and the blockade of its borders—the two most burning issues at the time. With the end of the ceasefire Hamas took up the firing of rockets at Israeli border towns. Israeli politicians (facing a parliamentary election in February) then decided on a "forceful response," which included Israeli fighter jets dropping bombs over Gaza—the war was a reality. At the end of January 2009 there was a *de facto* ceasefire even if some rockets were also fired at southern Israel from Gaza, answered by Israeli bombings of southern Gaza. This was a pattern that threatened to repeat itself under the current situation.

A tit-for-tat way of interacting is characteristic for the vicious circles that often appear in Israeli-Palestinian relations. Trying to pinpoint the causes of the conflict in a few lines is not easy. In the Gaza case it can be illustrated by the following chain of events:

> The reason is the Hamas movement firing Kassam-rockets against cities in Southern Israel, Hamas is firing the rockets because there is an Israeli blockade against Gaza, and the Israeli blockade exists because Hamas has one Israeli soldier as prisoner, and Hamas has one Israeli prisoner because there are hundreds of Palestinian prisoners in Israel and Israel has . . .

Of course, the focus one needs to take should be decided by the problem under discussion in order to make a meaningful analysis.

The outcome of the Gaza war can also be described by the huge destruction of property in Gaza and by statistics of individuals killed and injured on both sides.[19] Furthermore, infrastructure and property has

18. This example is illustrated by information from Israeli and Palestinian sources, mainly on the Internet.

19. "Gaza: at least 1,300 killed, at least 410 of them children and 104 women. Over 5,320 injured, over 350 of them severely injured (Palestinian Ministry of Health figures). Israel: 3 civilians and 10 soldiers killed. Over 84 civilians injured, 4 of them severely injured, not including those treated for shock. 113 soldiers injured, of them one in critical

been destroyed on an enormous scale. Both sides in the war are accused by civil society organizations of violating International Humanitarian Law and human rights, and of committing war crimes.

Israeli civil society organizations accuse the Israeli military forces of committing grave violations of International Humanitarian Law and call for urgent humanitarian action.

> In addition, Israel is also hitting civilian objects, having defined them as "legitimate military targets" solely by virtue of their being "symbols of government."[20]

The military activities are named in the call for action as an example of disproportionate harm to civilians. B'tselem accuses Israel of holding many Palestinian Gaza prisoners for days in harsh, humiliating, and degrading conditions and threatening their lives and their health. The detainees also included minors who were handcuffed and blindfolded. They were held for days in pits dug in the ground near tanks and in combat areas.[21] The transfer of Palestinians detained by Israeli forces to an army camp for detention of "unlawful combatants" reinforces concerns for the fundamental human rights of those detainees.[22] Amnesty International accuses Israel of a widespread use of the chemical white phosphorus. The phosphorus has been spread in densely populated residential areas in Gaza, thus targeting Palestinian civilians.[23]

---

condition and 20 suffering moderate or severe injuries". Human Rights in Gaza & Israel. Online: http://gazaeng.blogspot.com.

20. "Clear and present danger to the lives and well-being of tens of thousands of civilians," B'Tselem, January 14, 2009. Online: http://www.btselem.org/english/press_releases/20090114.asp. Behind the open letter were several organizations: Adalah—The Legal Center For Arab Minority Rights In Israel, Amnesty International Israel Section, Bimkom—Planners For Planning Rights, B'Tselem—The Israeli Information Center For Human Rights In The Occupied Territories, Gisha—Legal Center For Freedom Of Movement, Hamoked—Center For Defence Of The Individual, Physicians For Human Rights—Israel Public Committee Against Torture In Israel, Yesh Din—Volunteers For Human Rights.

21. "Israel held many Gaza prisoners in harsh and humiliating conditions and threatened their lives and their health," B'tselem, January 28, 2009. Online: http://www.btselem.org/English/Press_Releases/20090128.asp.

22. "Public Statement on the Treatment of Detainees Taken During the Current War in Gaza," Public Committee against Torture in Israel, January 8, 2009. Online: http://www.stoptorture.org.il/en/node/1368.

23. "Time for accountability in Gaza and southern Israel," Amnesty International, January 26. Online: http://www.amnesty.org/en/appeals-for-action/time-accountability-gaza-and-southern-israel.

Accusations have been directed against Hamas for conducting extra-judicial executions of alleged Palestinian collaborators.[24] Hamas, as well as other Palestinian armed groups, are also accused of firing rockets indiscriminately into population centers, killing several Israeli civilians.[25]

In a situation of at least a temporary ceasefire, the questions concerning accusations of war crimes appear on the agenda. To what degree have there been war crimes from both sides? Has there been an extensive disproportionate use of military force by Israel? In cases of war crimes, should the responsible be put on trial in Israel or on an international tribunal? And what to do with those responsible in Gaza?

The UN Fact Finding Mission on the Gaza Conflict, under the leadership of Justice Richard Goldstone, had the mandate to investigate all violations of international human rights law and International Humanitarian Law that might have been committed. Conclusions of the 575-page report to the UN General Assembly demonstrated that Israel committed serious violations of international human rights and humanitarian law in Gaza and that the Israeli actions were "amounting to war crimes, and possibly crimes against humanity."[26] The same goes for the armed Palestinian groups in Gaza, who were also committing war crimes and possibly crimes against humanity.

In its conclusions the report states:

> From the facts gathered, the Mission found that the following grave breaches of the Fourth Geneva Convention were committed by the Israeli armed forces in Gaza: wilful killing, torture or inhuman treatment, wilfully causing great suffering or serious injury to body or health, and extensive destruction of property, not justified by military necessity and carried out unlawfully and wantonly. As grave breaches these acts give rise to individual criminal responsibility. The Mission notes that the use of human

24. "Extra-judicial execution of alleged collaborators by Hamas," B'tselem, January 26, 2009. Online: http://www.btselem.org/English/Collaboration/20090126_Killing_of_Collaboration_Suspects_in_Gaza.asp.

25. "Time for accountability," Amnesty International.

26. "United Nations Fact Finding Mission on the Gaza Conflict," UN, September 29, 2009. Online: http://www2.ohchr.org/english/bodies/hrcouncil/specialsession/9/docs/HRCPressRelease29092009.doc.

shields also constitutes a war crime under the Rome Statute of the International Criminal Court.[27]

Palestinian armed groups still launch rockets into southern Israel and the Israeli soldier has still not been released. For the Palestinian population in the Gaza Strip the situation is very severe with little of reconstruction being possible, and the standoff continues with blockades and isolation. Israel continues with air strikes into Gaza.

TIMOR-LESTE

Timor-Leste is the eastern part of the island Timor, which is located north of Australia and is one of many in a chain of islands between Java and New Guinea. It was a Portuguese colony from 1512 and Portugal was in control of the territory up to 1974, when it unilaterally left Timor-Leste without a final settlement being reached of the question of its political future. The population in Timor-Leste in the 1970s was around 800,000–900,000, and it is about the same today. Timor-Leste is Asia's poorest country, depending to a high degree on international assistance for its budget. At the same time, the country has large reserves of oil and gas, on-shore and off-shore (in the Timor Sea between Australia and Timor-Leste), and is preparing itself for a more active role in the extraction of these resources. Besides this, the main exports of Timor-Leste are coffee, rice, and some marble.

Timor-Leste was ill-prepared to take destiny into its own hands when Portugal left in 1974. While the political groups—"parties" were not really formed at the time—were unprepared for the Portuguese exodus, civil society had difficulties to expressing itself very well at the time, unless it was related to the Catholic Church in Timor-Leste or to any part of the state administration that was accepted or promoted by the Indonesian authorities.

An internal conflict developed between groups with different approaches to the process of self-determination itself, leading to short civil war. This internal conflict was anchored in social, economic and traditional patterns of values and control in Timor-Leste, and related to more local dimensions than the international status issue that was dealt with by the United Nations and which drew international attention. The internal conflict was basically over the relationship with Indonesia: should

27. *Human Rights in Palestine*, 417.

Timor-Leste opt for self-determination in hopes for independence or should it seek some form of integration/autonomy within Indonesia?

After the short civil war between the two major political groups at the time—Fretilin and UDT[28]—Indonesia invaded Timor-Leste in December 1975. In 1976 it was annexed as a province of Indonesia and it was not until early 1999 that the Indonesian president at the time, B. J. Habibie, announced that Indonesia was ready for a Timor-Leste popular consultation—a referendum—over its future status. Following the Asian economic crises, demands had been too strong for Indonesia to resist regarding the issue of Timor-Leste's future.[29] As a consequence, the UN arranged a referendum in August 1999 in Timor-Leste, which resulted in a vote of 78.5 percent in favor of independence and 21.5 percent in favor of autonomy within Indonesia. It seems most groups in Timor-Leste expected this outcome; only Indonesia was surprised.

The outcome resulted in widespread looting, killing, and destruction by Indonesia-supported militia groups inside Timor-Leste, during a few weeks in September 1999. This lead to an international reaction and the deployment of, at its peak, 11,000 troops in Timor-Leste to restore security (INTERFET[30]). This force also prepared the ground for the UN Transitional Administration Timor-Leste (UNTAET), which functioned from 1999 to 2002 as the governing body of Timor-Leste. UNTAET basically set up the administration of a new state. Until today it is the most widely mandated UN mission. It was headed by the late Sergio Vieira de Mello.

The United Nations managed the conflict in Timor-Leste from a decolonization perspective. The issue for the world organization was to safeguard Timor-Leste's right to execute an act of self-determination and also assist in executing it. Timor-Leste was one of the last territories to be decolonized, thus it was the territory's future international status that was to be determined, in this case through the process of a referendum. Timor-Leste became an independent state on May 20, 2002.

28. Timor Democratic Union (UDT), Revolutionary Front for an Independent Timor-Leste (Fretilin).

29. A contributing factor to this development was the Nobel Peace Prize in 1996 to Msg. Carlos Belo, Bishop in Dili, Timor-Leste, and José Ramos-Horta, international spokesperson for the united Timorese resistance (CNRT).

30. International Force Timor-Leste (INTERFET), composed by troops/personnel from Australia, New Zealand, Malaysia, the Philippines, and another fourteen countries.

There are two dimensions where human rights and peace-building overlap in modern Timor-Leste history. The first relates to the history of Indonesian occupation: the cooperation of some residents of Timor-Leste with the Indonesian authorities there. The Indonesian occupation in Timor-Leste was extremely severe—in little more than a decade about a quarter of the total population lost their lives through killings and combat. In addition, Indonesia controlled and supported the militia groups that were formed in late 1990s as a response to the increasing demands for self-determination inside and outside Timor-Leste. These militias were particularly active in 1999 and it is estimated that about 70 percent of all buildings in the capital of Dili were destroyed from the looting and burning of houses, and the uprising of the militias in the wake of the publication of the results of the referendum in early September 1999.

The second dimension relates to the atrocities and violations of human rights that took place from the first years of internal conflict (before but also after the Indonesian occupation) and into the last months before the 1999 referendum. In the first phase of this twenty-five-year period these atrocities were often related to the pro-independence groups, while in the last phase of this period the situation was the opposite—the pro-autonomy groups were mostly affiliated with those that violated fundamental human rights. It should be noted that this double responsibility—in principle—was a historic circumstance that made it less problematic, from a political point of view, to form a commission for truth and reconciliation: no side could unilaterally blame the other for sole responsibility for atrocities. The difference in type and magnitude of the various violations that took place in this period is developed in the report of the commission.[31]

Livelihood and Confidence Issues

As is illustrated by this figure, there are two clusters of issues that go together in the Timor-Leste society of today. One is dealing with security, unemployment, and lack of economic interest; the other with the lack of confidence in the state administration and justice systems, upon which

---

31. See the two-thousand-page report *Chega!*.

is added a lack of "feeling" for what it means to be a Timor-Leste citizen in the first place.[32]

FIGURE 9: Reinforcing Issues in the Timor-Leste Situation

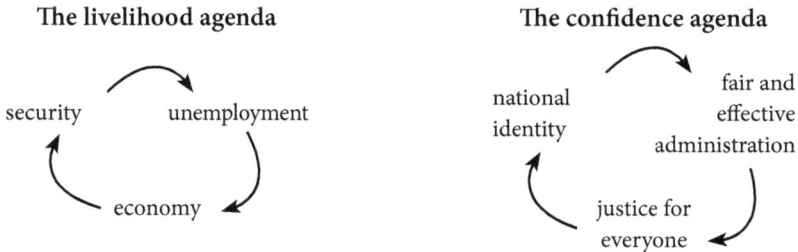

The livelihood agenda

security unemployment

economy

The confidence agenda

national identity

fair and effective administration

justice for everyone

The two agendas above represent different sectors of the civil society in Timor-Leste. The Livelihood agenda is represented by the private sectors of the civil society and it is critical to the lack of security (for investment) and its consequences. For instance, it is no wonder that unemployment continues on a high level and that the economy never creates an internal dynamic under such conditions. The Confidence agenda is pursued by some church leaders, by high-ranking civil society leaders inside or outside the parties, and some academics as well, who all realize that as long as "everyone" thinks more about his/her home region than the country as a whole, development will be partial and geographically haphazard in Timor-Leste.

This is where Timor-Leste stands today: with a legacy of serious crimes, but with no internal capacity to deal with it; and with a strongly felt need for development, but with no resources (human or economic) to initiate it. With a strong focus on one of these sides, the other one risks becoming secondary, and no one wants that, in principle. This is Timor-Leste's version of the problem of competing agendas of human rights and peace-building.

From the Horizon of the NGOs

The resistance years—as mentioned, from 1974 to 1999—created reﬂ gional and local networks within the civil society in Timor-Leste. Often the purpose was to support the resistance or to organize food distribu-

---

32. This final observation can be related to the idea mentioned above, that Timor-Leste is—or was—a society better organised locally or regionally, than nationally.

tion. This system made Timor-Leste, in practice, a country better organized on the regional and local levels than on the national level. From Portuguese times, and throughout the Indonesian occupation, Timor-Leste developed a critical view—at best—vis-à-vis the central authorities in Dili and elsewhere. This is something that today, under independence and otherwise very different conditions, can be both a useful and problematic experience during the development of the old and the new local civil society emerging in Timor-Leste.

With this history in mind the conclusion shall not be that the society of Timor-Leste is not a vibrant civil society today. There are many local organizations, some completely national, others with an international support, and others with an origin outside Timor-Leste. Timor-Leste in one sense has a different experience compared to the other cases discussed in this report: there is no "surviving" political class in the new independent state that reminds the population of the period before the war or before the conflict. In those days, either Indonesians or Timor-Leste nationals ruled Timor-Leste under Indonesian supervision. While some of these are now active in Timor-Leste, they do not constitute a political group with interests that need to be balanced in a new political system. Instead, they can form political parties, as can all other groups, if they are to organize themselves. For this reason, the political tensions that exist today are between different versions of independence policy, developed by former pro-independence politicians in the "old days."

Reconciliation on the Agenda?

When the smoke and sound of the looting and violence of September and October 1999 had disappeared, a discussion broke out between the Catholic Church and the winning side in the referendum in Timor-Leste: What is the proper place of reconciliation after an experience such as that in Timor-Leste? The political umbrella movement, CNRT[33], was interested in pursuing a South Africa-style reconciliation commission, which could once and for all, and relatively quickly, treat the atrocities and sometimes very serious crimes that had taken place.

A famous exchange of views was emerging at the time between the CNRT leader, Xanana Gusmâo, who advocated "reconciliation first, justice then"—on the basis that without reconciliation, justice faces the

33. National Council of Timorese Resistance.

risk of becoming vengeance—and the bishop and Nobel Prize Laureate Carlos Belo, who took the opposite view: "justice first, then reconciliation." In the end, the international community established a Serious Crimes Panel with national and international judges and also a national truth and reconciliation commission, which used a traditional and often-practiced community reconciliation mechanism, sometimes called Badame, as part of its methods, but only for less serious crimes.

This development illustrates another dimension of the relations between human rights and peace-building. Timor-Leste's particular predicament is that the worst atrocities, and the most responsible individuals, were committed by persons that no longer are to be found inside Timor-Leste but in Indonesia, and thus are outside of reach of the Timor-Leste justice system. Obviously Timor-Leste could ask for their extradition. This would at the same time raise a number of politically sensitive issues since some of these persons in Indonesia are still very powerful and influential in a country with which Timor-Leste needs to have the best possible relations. Moreover, the legal system of Timor-Leste would not be able to deal with them on a national level. It still has a long way to go to be developed in terms of competence and logistics.

For the moment, the Timor-Leste government has taken a soft position vis-à[<grave accent]-vis Indonesia on this matter and abstained from demands of extradition. Instead, together with Indonesia it has organized a commission of truth and friendship between the two countries. This commission, which has been criticized by many international organizations including the UN for a toothless and human rights–provoking mandate, produced a report that rejected propositions for amnesty and instead described and analyzed numerous violations and developments between the two countries during the Indonesian period of occupation.[34]

In the end, Timor-Leste faces a number of issues that relate to each other, which are still under development. New patterns of cooperation and conflict are developing and the civil society is part of the formation and formulation of these issues.

34. See "The Commission on Truth and Friendship," War Crimes Studies Center, http://socrates.berkeley.edu/~warcrime/Truth_commission.html.

ISSUES RAISED BY THE COUNTRY CASES

The five cases analyzed here—Colombia, the Democratic Republic of Congo, Guatemala, Palestine, and Timor-Leste—represent not only different historical experiences but also different types of relations between the Human Rights and Peace-Building agendas. Some situations are focused on a few principles and methods of action, others concern broad approaches to a multitude of questions and challenges. It is obvious that we are dealing with a combination of human rights and peace-building factors that need to be identified and clarified further in order to understand how a constructive relationship between the two might be established.

Some of the five country cases have reached a point of agreement/ peace, some have not. In the cases of Colombia, Palestine, and the DRC, there are partial or, as some would prefer to say, failing attempts at making peace—in Colombia in 1991 (new constitution), in Palestine in 1993 (Oslo Accords), and in the DRC in 1999 (Lusaka Accord). In the case of Timor-Leste and Guatemala there are agreements for a mechanism (referendum in 1999 in Timor-Leste) or a peace agreement (Guatemala 1996).

Depending on where a country is in the long process from war to peace, different human rights and peace-building issues are raised. Let us try to get an overview of the various elements in the processes that are under study here, based on the case presentations above.

Figure 12 below indicates in the phase each of the five country cases has reached. Each case has its human rights and peace-building problems. The logical step from this overview would then be to identify *what is typical for the issues at stake in each phase*, and later on, how can these issues be related to each other.

In all the five cases there are organizations and institutions working with either human rights or peace-building issues and a few of them aspire to work with both simultaneously. Even if the organizational structures vary, the issues are basically recurring, in different ways, in all the cases. From the five cases concerning civil society we can both draw conclusions and formulate general questions for further reflection, in this analysis and beyond its pages.

FIGURE 10: Five Country Situations—An Overview

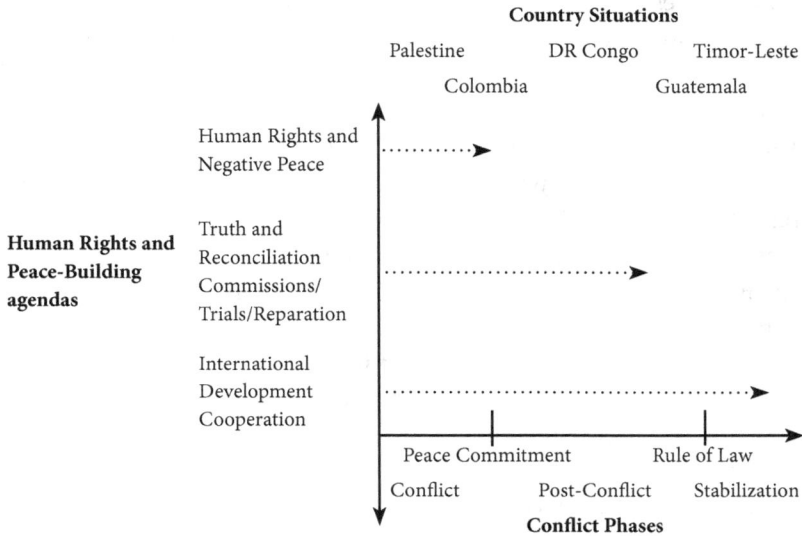

Country Situations

Palestine   DR Congo   Timor-Leste

Colombia   Guatemala

Human Rights and Peace-Building agendas

Human Rights and Negative Peace

Truth and Reconciliation Commissions/ Trials/Reparation

International Development Cooperation

Peace Commitment   Rule of Law

Conflict   Post-Conflict   Stabilization

Conflict Phases

In the case of Colombia the civil society is in many ways vibrant and active. It functions on all levels of society and sometimes plays a vital role even for national processes. At the same time it is pressured by the implications of the conflict(s) in the country and by the polarization that has grown significantly on all levels as a result of these situations.

If we continue to the Democratic Republic of Congo, it is a huge and not politically unified country. Instead different political groups make up ruling elites in different parts of the country. (This is not unique— Colombia is a case in point—but it is important for conflict and human rights analysis.) Coming to the eastern part of Congo, there is a clear lack of state presence and, at the same time, a growing civil society taking on in the midst of chaos and extreme violence from military factions.

The critical question for the Guatemalan civil society, as well as for the country as a whole, is still centered on the issues that dominated the peace process, namely land, democratic rights, and identity-based rights. In addition, the lack of justice, both during and after the civil war, adds to this deficit. There is one major difference from the peace process situation: the experience of having a peace process, with its implications for hope, trust, and the reconstruction of lives and society.

Turning to the Palestinian situation, the mere analysis of the situation requires a complex approach combining history with local realities and power asymmetries of wider global interest. The occupation of the Palestinian Territories—which is a fact established by international legal bodies—is carried out in a way that violates international law, for instance through limiting Palestinians' lives and work. It puts a definitive mark on all kinds of activities taken by the civil society in the Palestinian areas. The internal Palestinian situation, with its international repercussions, in its turn does not make this situation easier.

Finally, the case of Timor-Leste is complex in being colonized by Portugal, occupied by Indonesia, and between 1999 and 2002 transformed by the UN (UNTAET) into an independent state. The shift over the centuries from a dependency approach to politics to an *in*dependency approach is demanding. One question for civil society is why independence and democracy did not bring wealth, at least after some years. How can the international community and some national NGOs be asking for "justice" for perpetrators and victims when a whole population is unjustly treated by the same international community, and when a life in prison is more protected from starvation than a "free" person?

Countries in conflict and with grave human rights violations sooner or later become polarized as part of a mobilization over the conflict issues. This is certainly true in the cases of Colombia, Guatemala, Palestine, and Timor-Leste. It is true for Eastern Congo (DRC) as well, most clearly in the perspective of the Lusaka Agreement, the internal conflict and genocide in Rwanda in the 1990s, and its repercussions in DRC.

Given this situation, to what extent is it possible for a civil society—as peace-building organizations—to function as a connector and bridge-building mechanism in a polarized society? And to what extent is it possible for a civil society—as human rights organizations—to work for all to have the same rights and address how to bring perpetrators to justice? From our perspective it seems to be a joint task for both human rights and peace-building organizations in their efforts to build peace and a just society. But is it uncontroversial to claim it is a joint task?

A major theme in these five cases has also been that hopes and aspirations raised by peace agreements, partial agreements, etc. seldom become realized. On the contrary, for people living in the areas of concern the abuses and violations of human rights continue, and little has been changed in comparison to the pre-conflict situation.

A common question in several of the cases is if there are still ways and means—hopefully peaceful—that can be used to achieve a change of land rights, land use, and land development—or is it the case that the country is doomed to remain in the glaringly unjust system that remains after the conflict, just as it did before?

Let us keep these questions in mind as a background to the specific search for bridging the two agendas in the following chapters.

4

The Third Agenda

INTRODUCING THE THIRD AGENDA

B RIEFLY SPEAKING, HUMAN RIGHTS is about relations between rights
holders and duty bearers, and peace-building is about transforming
conflicts into peaceful and durable relations between parties and victims
and their wider society.

As we have seen, the two agendas' historic and organizational developments have—for good reasons—led to their institutionalization, for
instance via the state system (including the United Nations) or through
civil society organizations. In addition, the realization of these ideas is
often the result of interplay between states and the civil society.

If we utilize the fact that the relationship between the agendas is
close, due to normative and contextual conditions, we will find possibilities to develop more substantial and deeper relations. This chapter
argues that this is possible.

We are interested here in the extent to which ideas from the respective agendas can be applied and made relevant in a way that utilizes the
particular qualities of each of them. We also investigate if the agendas can
go beyond their present limits and develop some original initiatives.

One point of departure for this study is that the discussion and
friction between the agendas are not about their utility or relevance
in principle, neither of the Human Rights nor of the Peace-Building
Agenda. Our concern is not to address those that question the agendas as
agendas. The point of departure is instead that the relationship between
the agendas could and should be *complementary, interdependent, and of
mutual respect for their unique characters.* Therefore we are interested in
identifying approaches where the qualities of the agendas are applied,

not only as such, but also in a way that enhances their capacity *beyond* what would be possible if they were only applied unilaterally.

From this point of departure, the discussion becomes: "what is relevant, and when?" It is about *methods and applicability of principles in certain situations and process phases.* This is the key idea behind what is suggested here and will be called a *Third agenda.* Through applying competences within the two original agendas additional actions can be undertaken, some of which would not be possible by one agenda alone. As we shall see, the Third agenda includes both separate and coordinated initiatives, joint actions, and new approaches.

To organize systematic inventories of principles and areas of effective integration and/or mutual cooperation—locally, nationally, and internationally—is perhaps the most conspicuous step in a better use of the potential that the two agendas represent. This does not imply changing norms or principles, but requires some methodological (re-)considerations. Such an inventory is a central part of what could be a Third agenda. This can range from training to advocacy, from local lobby work to (inter-)national campaigns. Such an approach does not, however, and should not, exclude separate activities.

Even if this is worthwhile in itself, is it a challenge to go one step further? If so, one would reach a point where it is possible to construct combinations of the (traditional) actions/projects of the two agendas that in the Third agenda are now carried out within a *comprehensive framework* that would create conditions that each agenda unilaterally is not able to produce. This is then a way to create synergy effects between the existing Human Rights and Peace-Building agendas.

A Way Forward

In this chapter we will present the various aspects of the Third agenda step by step, facing the risk of making the text heavy at some points. This will be done in the following way.

First, we introduce the *basic categories* of analysis, including a proposal for a new category of actors. Second, the characteristics of *three phases*—conflict, post-conflict, and stabilization phases—in which both challenges and actions are formulated and undertaken by the agendas. Third, we propose *methodological approaches* for actions and initiatives based on the two agendas. As a fourth ingredient, in this palette of aspects, we introduce some illustrating *concepts of change*, in order to show

how the linking and development of relations between the agendas can take place.

WHO IS INVOLVED?

Parties, Victims, Duty bearers, and Rights holders

Important for understanding conflict as well as post-conflict situations is of course the parties involved—including their interests, positions, and actions. Equally important are individuals and groups exposed to violations of human rights—their suffering, victimization, and the duty bearers' responsibility, etc. *Parties, victims, rights holders,* and *duty bearers* are fundamental categories in the analysis of conflict and its development into peaceful relations.

Party is in this study a concept for those that over time organize themselves for a political purpose and who employ certain means (peaceful or violent) to realize their political aims. *Victim* as a concept is by many considered a "passive" or "reductive" concept, especially when applied in a long-term context. This view has some merit, but in relation to being a perpetrator's target, "victim" is, we believe, an appropriate description. In some situations, the concepts of "survivor," "exposed," or "targeted" are used to avoid an association to passivity. In this study we will use the concept of "victim" as close to the victim-perpetrator situation as possible, but without claiming full consistency.

The concepts *rights holders* and *duty bearers* are closely linked to a human rights–based approach and the first concept depicts the rights of an individual or individuals jointly, as a group, who are entitled to claim rights. The latter concept refers to the responsible authorities' obligations of respecting, promoting, defending, and fulfilling the human rights.

While *parties* refer to the political aspect of the situation, *duty bearers* signifies a formal responsibility that is connected (in most cases) to the state, irrespective of whether it is a party or not. In internal armed conflicts, states are normally involved in the conflict and they are therefore often sitting on two chairs. On one hand they are legally bound to defend human rights and on the other they are politically bound to counter violence, something that in practice can easily come into conflict with human rights. In many cases this is something that is impossible to do without violating human rights or the laws of armed conflict.

In some situations the categories mentioned above may overlap—groups as well as individuals can in complex situations belong to different categories, not the least during the different processes of a conflict.

It is important to make the observation that the human rights discourse has its focus and departure in the rights and interests of the individual, while, at the same time, the peace-building discourse includes, not simply builds on, collective forms of organization in a community whether as parties, civil society organizations or other collective units. It is one of the advantages of the Third agenda that it combines and gives attention to both individual and collective needs and interests.

Conflict-Formed Actors

For the situations that are addressed in this study, we have observed that there is a need for a new category to be introduced in order to have an adequate representation of all acting and relevant segments of a society in conflict and post-conflict situations. This category is here called *conflict-formed actors*.

Conflict and war, in particular when protracted, shake up fundamental social structures. After some time, and often without being directly involved in the conflict, people (need to) find new ways and means of living because of the conflict. Based on new relations and new expressions of interest and action groups and new structures are created—characterized by necessity and adaption to new conditions. Let us look at some categories and examples of conflict-formed actors:

- critics: anti-conflict NGOs, victims' associations; peace communities, NGOs working in conflict areas
- adaptors: farmers changing crops, markets moving to safe areas
- gainers: companies supplying the parties or gaining from war conditions, narco-traffickers arms traders, human traffickers

As the list of examples show, some conflict-formed actors come from within the conflict, others have been outside all the time. Obviously, the work of NGOs, the Red Cross, religious organizations, and other institutions that began before the conflict is also likely to be changed by the conflict. However, these organizations do not originate from the conflict's impact and in case of a substantial peace process, and they can return to other matters within their respective specific agendas.

By recognizing this, we see that there is a category of actors[1] which is formed by the *conflict process itself*. Some of them look upon their work as being temporary, while others take a semi-permanent approach to what is seen as an unavoidable development. As we have mentioned, here we find individuals or groups that change their daily "normal" life so as to relate to the conflict in—as they see it—an as appropriate way as possible. As we shall see, this has potential implications for the conflict's development, for the peace process as a whole, as well as for the parties. In particular we shall study the potential outcomes that arise for conflict-formed actors in the peace process.

Members in this category relate in different ways to different parties in a conflict, as well as to victims, rights holders, and duty bearers. In addition, some of them may just prefer to avoid the conflict completely by leaving conflict-ridden areas, not as forcefully displaced people, but as part of conscious planning. If they stay, they may move the location of, for instance, their business to an area where they can make profit from the needs of the fighting parties. They may even sell weapons or change the production of food so as to fit new market conditions. Another type of conflict-formed actor is those that mobilize against the conflict, including the whole sphere of NGOs working for peace and human rights. They are conflict-formed actors if they were started by the ongoing conflict itself.[2] Other groups have simply become more or less "paralyzed bystanders"—they are onlookers, or possibly even tactically cooperative with a human rights–violating regime in order to avoid problems.

One segment of conflict-formed actors is made up of those that resist the conflict by showing and practicing alternatives; they choose to live outside the conflict.[3] Some of them demonstrate clearly that "peace is possible" and that there are alternatives to the conflict's divisions. This

---

1. An actor influences a process without constituting its driving force, either directly or indirectly. A conflict party, on the other hand, is constitutive of a conflict and is then analytically different from actors in a society living with conflict. Without parties there can be no conflict, but actors need not be parties.

2. At the end of the Cold War, the difference between conflict-formed actors and other civil society movements was clearly visible in Europe, for instance, when movements against deterrence and the arms race were put in a position of losing their clear position of opposition. Other peace movements continued on the basis of other issues.

3. See Valenzuela *Neutrality in Internal Armed Conflicts*.

kind of group should not be mixed up with what is often called the "secondary party" in a conflict analysis language.[4]

Another segment of the conflict-formed actors are those that during the conflict have been exposed to challenging situations—maybe against their will and contrary to their planning—and who have had to take a stand from unprepared situations. Some of them might simply become passive "onlookers" or "bystanders" to serious violations of human rights, conflict behavior, etc. As time goes by and a conflict becomes protracted, this category of citizens will become larger and larger. In the end of the conflict process, their life and lack of action (or actions) will, along with the active parties, be part of a general discussion about responsibility, memory, and reconstruction. It is not until this last stage, particularly if members of this group are addressed individually, that they become actors in the process.

What all these groups have in common is their social role, including a possible responsibility and potential capacity to act for or against peace in a broad sense. They are defined by an intra-conflict process, something that needs to be analyzed through the conflict that they—maybe even against their will—have need to respond to.

Analytically speaking *conflict-formed actors* make up a fifth analytical category, besides *parties, rights holders, duty bearers*, and *victims*, to be used alongside with them when relevant.

WHEN TO UNDERTAKE ACTION?

In a process of moving from "war" to "peace"—to put it simply—there are qualitative developments that change the conditions for implementing human rights as well as peace-building. Such critical developments produce substantially different situations. Since they are not fixed but are "floating," we will call them *phases*. We will use them here to describe how the Third agenda can be useful in each of them. The phases focus some specific characteristics of each period. Most important is the insight *that a phase is neither a fixed state of affairs nor a clear-cut time period of certain conditions*. Instead, a phase is used here as a concept for representing a set of common social features that, taken together, make

---

4. A secondary party is a party that supports primary parties in a conflict, and does so with a particular solution in mind. The support can be of different types, of course.

up the conditions under which various Third agenda initiatives will be effective.

Complex societies, often with a violent past and with an unstable political leadership, can drift between various phases. Some of them may have almost all the conditions related to an ongoing armed conflict, while others are relatively stable even if there is no formal agreement signed. We will, for reasons of clarity, treat the phases as separate entities and present them according to a timeline in order to discuss the conditions of each specific situation.

To make this even more complex, it is not only that situations come and go for they may also be regionally different within a country. One region can have relative stability for a long period while another may never achieved this even if a civil war, for instance, has stopped.

We would argue that there are two qualitative turning points in a process from war to peace that make a fundamental difference and thereby create very obvious phases. We call the first one the *peace commitment*, which is the type of change that brings a society from ongoing armed violence to a situation in which the use of violence would be seen—by one or more parties—as breaking a commitment of some kind. This can be everything from unilaterally declared ending of violence from parties to an agreed cease-fire or a full peace agreement—or just an implicit agreement of change.

The second turning point comes with the end of a period of transformation and the introduction of a stable society. This means, for instance, the ending of special war crime panels and constitutional or security sector reforms (SSR). All of these have a limited period of implementation. Going from this phase of transitional mechanisms to a permanent and stabilizing process is termed here the introduction of the *rule of law*.

As noted above, these situations do not cover the whole conflict process. They focus only on its final stages—from the ending of an open, ongoing armed conflict to the stabilization of a society after dealing with this conflict. A full "conflict circle" is not included in this analysis; instead it addresses situations wherein the tension between the two agendas up till now has been most visible.

From the beginning it also needs to be said that peace processes—like any social process—rarely unfold in a single direction; setbacks, returns to the "status quo ante," etc. are not uncommon and are part of the changing conditions that any social process presents. This feature of such processes does not invalidate the utility of figures and concepts that try to highlight what is typical for different phases, the role of the Third agenda, and their relationship within a larger whole.

In order to create a representative structure of this gradual process from war to peace, for practical and theoretical reasons we have made a simple, but still open, division of this process into three phases: the *conflict* phase, the *post-conflict* phase, and the *stabilization* phase.

FIGURE 11: Phases in Focus

1. CONFLICT PHASE		
ONGOING VIOLENCE AND WAR	OCCUPATION	GENOCIDE
Peace Commitment		
2. POST-CONFLICT PHASE TRANSFORMATION		
Rule of Law		
3. STABILIZATION PHASE TOWARDS NORMALIZATION		

The conflict phase can have many levels, obviously. It can even develop into a permanent occupation—intentional or consequential— or, at worst, into genocide and other crimes against humanity. The turning point between the *conflict* and *post-conflict* phase is, as mentioned above, the *peace commitment*. The *post-conflict* phase is the middle phase and, as we shall see, it connects to both the conflict's history (memory and transitional issues) and to the future (reconstruction). This is a transformative social process.

The *stabilization phase*, finally, is at hand when transitional arrangements are not used any more: the country is returned to the *rule of law* according to a permanent judiciary system and politically the former conflict—if it is not solved—is treated within a functioning democratic framework that does not threaten the daily security and stability of the country.[5]

A question that consistently arises in this context—and which we will not dwell on here—is, of course, whether human rights is a precondition for peace—wide or narrow peace—or if it is the other way around; without at least a minimum of peace, no human rights protection can be maintained. Maybe this is just a too simple way of addressing the question. What does the relationship between the two look like? This is a critical question. It will be present in all three phases and through the rest of this study. We will now proceed with a presentation of the three phases.

The Conflict Phase

The conflict phase is the initial phase under study in this project. The characteristics of this phase can be summarized as having three dimensions: the issue at stake, the actions of the parties, and the motivations and attitudes towards each other that the parties have.

A conflict phase is a phase where violations of human rights are intensified in comparison to the situation before the conflict started. For sure, there is most likely a pre-existing history of tension, violence, and previous violations of human rights. The introduction of violence in a conflict means, however, a qualitative increase in its brutality. The conflict phase is defined here by its direct violence—killings, armed actions, massacres—all of which take place as part of the fighting.

To give just a few examples this means, for instance, that military rule and authoritarian dictatorships—such as in Chile and Argentina in the 1970s, or Burma/Myanmar, Zimbabwe, and North Korea at the time of writing—are illustrations of such conflicts. In such situations violence is often at a low level, but repressive, targeted, and ruthless.

A second group of conflicts are civil wars, which are sometimes about controlling the government in order to change what is seen as an unjust political system or domination by one group over another, such as in Guatemala, Colombia, Liberia, Somalia, South Africa, the Congo (DRC), or Afghanistan.

---

5. After a stabilization phase, a consolidation phase is a natural step. However, from the perspective of this study's purpose, such a possible phase is not significantly different from the stabilization phase.

Other civil wars are made up of the conflicts that challenge the present state, or the formation process of a state, often because minority rights are violated or national movements are not allowed to execute their right to self-determination.

There is—among the cases mentioned above—a group of conflicts that seem particularly difficult to settle. They are called protracted conflicts and represent situations where the parties somehow manage to live and develop in the midst of serious violence. Examples of such conflicts are India-Pakistan, Israel-Palestine, Colombia, Guatemala, and the Philippines.

Finally, some of the conflicts are particularly serious from a humanitarian point of view, such as the Congo (DRC), Somalia, Sudan, Sri Lanka, Afghanistan, Colombia, and Palestine.

The agenda in internal wars is in most cases related to failing protection of human rights. If unjust political systems, economies, and land rights dominate the issues, such issues are sometimes channeled into a traditional "left vs. right" conflict (such as in Guatemala, El Salvador, Nicaragua, and Colombia). In other cases, ethnic groups, often in a minority, feel their rights to identity are denied and suppressed in various ways. Some of these groups argue that an independent state of their own, or at least autonomy within their present state, could be a solution. Examples of this situation are Sudan, Sri Lanka, Aceh/Indonesia, the Philippines, Somalia, Nagorno-Karabakh, Kashmir, the breakup of Yugoslavia, and Cyprus. In a few cases, the conflict's background is related to the formation of states or an ongoing decolonization process, such as in the Middle East (Israel and Palestine), Timor-Leste, or Western Sahara. Also, the break-up of the apartheid system in South Africa is a paradigmatic change in a country with a colonial heritage, although taking place within an independent, sovereign state.

For the small category of conflicts *between* states, such as Russia vs. Georgia, the USA and Great Britain vs. Iraq, India vs. Pakistan, or Ethiopia vs. Eritrea, there are either power dimensions or national issues (such as one's own people in the other state). Sometimes this is defined as a boundary issue (Ecuador vs. Peru, Iran vs. Iraq) or as a matter of ideology and government (Iraq, Afghanistan, and also the 2009 Gaza War had this dimension).

States or non-state parties not following the rules of war according to the International Humanitarian Law are at risk of not only committing severe violations through using, for example, torture and extra-judicial killings, but also committing more severe crimes. The strength of military means used must be measured against the principle of proportionality, regulating that the exercise of power should not exceed that which is necessary to achieve the objective. Otherwise, the military activity may be considered a crime. The experience from several wars and violent conflicts, for instance in the Balkans and the DRC, tell about systematic use of rape and other forms of sexual violence that destroy the lives of the women targeted, but also aiming at the destruction of the entire social structure of society.

These are but examples that the limits of warfare have been exceeded. In such instances it has changed into a crime against humanity. Open violence and severe abuses can on some occasions be developed into genocide, crimes against humanity, war crimes, and crimes of aggression. A somewhat special case of armed conflict is that of occupation, which can include both internal and international dimensions.

The reasons for an occupation can be different: to control a population, to acquire land, to get control over natural resources, to achieve a security zone against an enemy, etc. Whatever reasons there may be, internationally agreed rules regulate what is allowed and what is prohibited for an occupying power in occupied territories. These measures are taken in order to protect the people and make a transfer of power back to the occupied people as smooth as possible. In the case of Timor-Leste, the United Nations arranged a referendum in August 1999 and the Indonesian occupation ended. Yet in Palestine, no UN (or other) efforts have ended the occupation that has lasted for more than four decades.

What characterizes the motivations and attitudes among parties in a conflict? To be in a conflict means to have a relationship—a hostile relationship. That is different from being isolated, because someone that is involved in a conflict gets impressions of the other and makes interpretations. Normally conflict produces simplifications, stereotypes, and unfounded negative views about the other side—it becomes part of the conflict and the fighting to avoid saying something "good" about the other side. Denigrating and false accusations are common in wartime. The personal integrity—which is a human right—of the enemy is neglected in times of conflict and war. All this, taken together, means that in a conflict truth becomes the first victim, and hate and anger its strongest feelings. Truth and conflict are—it seems—incompatible realities. For this reason, and as we shall see later, truth telling is an important aspect of a peace process. But also personal attitudes and the group mentality have to be reconstructed in order to find a point of constructive relations between former enemies.

As indicated above, the conflict phase has specific origins. It does not begin out of the blue. We will not go deeper into the many reasons behind conflicts here. A common way to think about conflict is that of a circular approach: grievances and violated human rights cause conflict, and an inconclusive settlement of that conflict sooner or later leads to new grievances and conflicts—in a never-ending and circular process.

We do not accept such a schematic approach. We believe that peace commitment that recognizes the issues at stake, together with an adequate protection of human rights related to these issues, can break a vicious circle. New conflicts can certainly arise over new issues, but that is another thing. This is what makes the peace-building aspect important: it has a focus on both norms and institutions—democratic, civil, and judicial—that "take care" of grievances and treat them in an equal and correct manner.

During the conflict phase, escalations come and go. Such waves depend on external factors, such as arms deliveries, political support, and economic contributions, as well as internal factors, such as recruitment of soldiers, stronger attacks from the enemy, and support from new groups in the society. Some types of escalations are not likely to return to the level before the escalation. Examples of this are horizontal escalation—i.e., new parties become involved—as well as vertical escalation: more/stronger weapons.

There are some established working methods to be used in conflict situations. We regard them as typical for either the Human Rights or the Peace-Building agenda, or both such as:

- conflict analysis;
- analysis of rights holders and duty bearers;
- getting an end to ongoing violence;
- "peace is possible";
- preparations for reconstruction;
- monitoring enabling respect and protection;
- opinion-building;

- capacity-building.

In relation to *occupation* there are also some approaches such as:

- protection during occupation;
- responsibility to protect.

In relation to *genocide* and other severe crimes the means are often:

- military intervention;
- humanitarian intervention.

Peace Commitment: Entering the Post-Conflict Phase

To reduce the level of violence, and ultimately get a cease-fire, is the first goal. In UN language it falls under the concept of *peace-making*. This means a stop to the fighting, a basis on which all the other activities that are needed to settle a conflict begin. In this way, according to the UN, peace-making can be both peaceful (negotiated, with or without mediators) and a matter of force. Peace—i.e., narrow peace—can be enforced by military and other means upon parties that do not respect calls for an end to violence. This can be made by, for instance, the UN Security Council. It is, or should be, a temporary measure. The transition from this situation into a politically stable situation is crucial.

The peace commitment has, in this study, the role of an indicator: it marks the qualitative shift of means in a political struggle, a change from a period of ongoing violence and armed conflict to a period where violence for political purposes is rejected. This shift is sometimes marked by a concrete peace agreement—a formal text signed and duly implemented—but it does not always come to such a formal conclusion. Sometimes there is only a cease-fire that is prolonged indefinitely and institutionalized through a UN presence (such as Cyprus). Other times there is not even a cease-fire: fighting stops and the status quo of a given day is made the concrete ending point of a conflict (such as the Second World War or the Korean conflict). The military defeat of the Tamil Tigers in Sri Lanka is, in this context, an interesting case because it is unusual for protracted civil wars to "end" through military campaigns.

Peace commitments can be expressed in different ways. Peace agreements—or comparable documents—are sometimes criticized for being vague, idealistic, incomplete, and/or backward-looking. This may be true for some agreements, since all these characteristics can be traced to the fact that peace agreements deal with conflict issues—matters that are troublesome and sometimes difficult and sensitive to deal with. Using "diplomatic" language, as lofty aspirations or general talk about friendship for instance, is one way of avoiding the difficult issues.

In reality, a peace agreement is a document signed between (former) enemies and designed to deal with the future. It refers to a situation where both parties are weakened and should outline a new power distribution between the parties, which did not fully achieve what they wanted on the battlefield.

Peace agreements are constitutive texts that establish a new order between (former) enemies. Since many conflicts in practice are rooted in violations of human rights, there are human rights principles, and often mechanisms and institutions, introduced as part of a peace agreement. Respect for human rights in such situations becomes the principle that solves the conflict. For instance, a mechanism for self-government (such as autonomy) may be the final settlement for a conflict over rights to identity, ethnicity, or religion. A typical case in point of this kind of conflict resolution is the peace agreement in Aceh, in Indonesia.

In brief, a comprehensive peace agreement should address the same dimensions of a conflict as the conflict analysis: its background and consequences, the issues at stake and their future regulation, the humanitarian consequences, and the institutionalization of a political system that is envisaged in the agreement.

The method and language of a peace agreement—formal or informal—is taken from the Peace-Building agenda. Based on the Human Rights agenda—not directly addressing peace agreements—it would be possible to claim that human rights violations are a cause, a symptom, or a reason behind the escalation of a violent conflict. This indicates that a direct Human Rights agenda can play an important role in establishing concrete agreements. Or put differently, without that agenda, the human rights situation—as well as the causes of the conflict—may not be solved.

Here is one possible area of conflict between the two agendas: one being "diplomatic" in order to be able to involve all parties and the other "naming" violations and perpetrators in order to be able to claim justice. In a sensitive part of negotiations it can for sure be problematic to take as a point of departure the accusation of parties as being perpetrators. But at the same time, there is a need to listen to the Human Rights agenda since it includes a parallel analysis—analysis of rights holders and duty bearers—of the conflict. And the question is: whose perspective should have priority, and when?

The Post-Conflict Phase

The post-conflict phase is a phase where the previous conflict—including its consequences in human and material terms—still dominates the activities of the (former) parties, the state and the civil society. This does not exclude peace-building and future-oriented activities, but what characterizes this phase is the still necessary, but temporary, treatment of the immediate effects of the recently finished armed conflict, such as refugees, internally displaced people, reconstruction, disarmament, demobilization and rehabilitation of soldiers, and implementation of the peace agreement (or equivalent).

The post-conflict phase is a crucial period for successfully establishing the peace as not just a temporary halt in the war, but as a permanent situation after the war. It is also possible to describe this time as a period in-between the end of direct fighting and the beginning of a process of stabilization and development. In this interim period, it is a key factor, in relevant cases, to establish a government as a transitional government respected by all parties in the conflict as well as by major actors in the civil society.

There will be a lot of questions related to the previous situation of violence and human rights abuses to be dealt with immediately after the cessation of hostilities. There is a need to find a solution for the victims, as well as for the groups still in arms in the ongoing conflict. Can any regular army continue as they did before the conflict? If the army represents a dictatorship of any kind there may be need for reconstruction and claiming responsibility for human rights violations. And what to do with ex-combatants from other parties, potentially representing a threat to security during the post-conflict phase, which raises questions concerning demobilization, disarmament, and reintegration? At the same time, ex-combatants may be victims—as in the case of child soldiers—who through bribes, force, or kidnapping have been enrolled into fighting forces.

Finally, this is a phase when the international interest on the media level—and therefore in the long run also from the donor community—is gradually reduced. This is a well-known fact. Yet at the same time, it is difficult to prepare for this and many NGOs, for instance, try to maintain the interest from the donor community in various ways.

In this phase, and as far as circumstances allow, there will also be initiatives that are genuinely new and that do not deal with the past conflict in any direct sense. To this category belong capacity-building (which is always a useful thing, whether after conflict or not), literacy campaigns, democratization, and health development. Normally the security sector has greater problems in "returning to the future" since its involvement in the past has been strong. Therefore, the civil society—even if seriously affected —may have a better point of departure than security agencies for its return to normal life through support from their regular institutions, such as churches/mosques/synagogues/temples, other existing civil society organizations, radio stations, schools, traditional leaders and social mechanisms, etc.

There are some established working methods to be used in post-conflict situations, i.e., the phase between a peace commitment and the rule of law. We regard them as typical for either the Human Rights or the Peace-Building agenda or both, and they include:

- peace dividend projects;
- accountability for the past;
- monitoring focusing on economic and social rights;
- building civil society capacity;
- transitional mechanisms;
- reconciliation;
- preparing for rule of law and civil society.

Rule of Law: Entering the Stabilization Phase

In order to enable a democratic society and the implementation of human rights, the rule of law is a central element. It is here used to indicate a turning point from a post-conflict society to a society that works on its internal and external stability. Thus it utilizes some fundamental state structures, such as a constitution, democratic legislature, and executive institutions. What in the previous phase were issues that at that time needed to be treated through temporary mechanisms—such as a transitional government, a constituent assembly, special courts dealing with the past, history/truth commissions, economic stabilization measures, and the like—are now managed through duly established state institutions. The rule of law establishes a basic degree of order to this development by giving the state legitimacy and the individual access to justice in a way that reflects, both in principle and practice, equality to all.

It has been argued that rule of law requires four necessary elements reflecting various instruments for governance:

> Democracy; proper legislation meeting relevant international standards; institutions to administer this law; and individuals with the necessary knowledge and integrity to handle this administration.[6]

Finally, it is necessary to make the observation that the elements mentioned in the quotation above may not all be introduced at the same time. This means that from a security perspective, for instance, a state can be in a post-conflict phase while it is legally or politically in a stabilization phase. In reality these branches of the state go together to some extent, but theoretically we need to see that there can be backlashes in one area while the rest of the system may function well, at least for a period of time.

For the purpose of this study, the change from a post-conflict phase—which actively deals with the past while at the same time tries to lay a groundwork for the future—into a stabilization phase indicates a shift where, relatively speaking, the past fades away and the future becomes a more important concern in public life as well as for the civil society and the nation as a whole.

The Stabilization Phase

From a long-term perspective this phase is the most important. We should remember that we still talk about a "phase" and not an endless situation. This phase ends when a society or a state is able to deal with all its matters without being limited or hampered by special considerations pertaining to the past conflict.

The phase following upon the post-conflict phase may still be characterized in the same terms as before the violent conflict. The violence

---

6. Corell, *Creating a Global Rule.*

has stopped and a transfer over to a stable society, with the implementation of human rights and peace-building, has been inaugurated. Still, human rights violations existing before the conflict are not necessarily solved. For example, the poor and landless people may still be marginalized. The poor as well as other groups still have little access to the instruments and institutions that may protect and implement their rights. If nothing further is done to the now stable situation, it can easily develop into a crisis again.

Now we give some examples of working methods typical for either the Human Rights or the Peace-Building agenda in the stabilization situation after rule of law has been introduced:

- human rights culture for rights holders and duty bearers;
- intercommunity trust-building;
- implementation of human rights;
- culture of democracy;
- democratic institutions;
- national minority protection.

As the case with the previously mentioned established methods, we refer to the continued discussion as *concepts for change*.

HOW TO USE THE THIRD AGENDA

A Third agenda would have as a fundamental, strategic starting point the identification of a *common working space* that forms a platform for joint action, for the sake of stability, enabling human rights protection and a peaceful development in general.

As a way of describing how the two agendas can relate to each other in a more effective way, we will discuss this with respect to three methodological approaches: *common assumption*, *integration*, and *twinning*. This is illustrated in Figure 12.

FIGURE 12: Types of Approaches in the Third Agenda

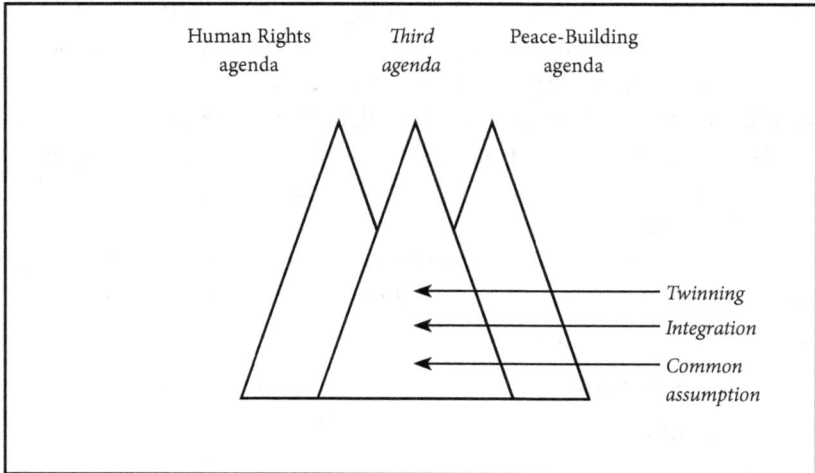

The three approaches represent a particular way of combining principles with practical initiatives in a peace-building or human rights framework. It is based on the idea that there is "no talk without action." When principles are put into practice, the theoretical rift that may have existed often evaporates since it becomes obvious that in reality the boundaries are porous between them. Therefore, the Third agenda needs concrete and visible activity that shows that "peace pays" and that human rights "makes a difference" to what the situation was before.

Common Assumption—Joining Principles

The two agendas represent fundamental, universal norms and ideas. With the *common assumption* approach we basically talk about a fundamental principle that can be embraced by both agendas. For each phase we will propose a different common determining factor that enables the two agendas to act in common as a Third agenda.

Integration—Making a New Blend

In international organizations like the UN, and also the OECD and within civil society organizations, a discussion is going on about how to relate the two agendas to each other if only by identifying commonalities and distinctions between them in order for them not to collide in their fieldwork. In the civil society, with organizations mainly working either with peace-building or with human rights, the question about the two agendas is on the increase. Today organizations appear with the intention of working with both agendas simultaneously. In some cases it is obvious that what is happening is that one of the agendas is added to an already existing one in practice. A human rights–based approach will then, at best, support the peace-building—or the other way around. In this spirit, the obvious way forward would be not to work against each other, but to work in an as integrated way as possible whenever there is a chance. The Third agenda would then be to *recognize the two agendas' different qualities* and develop an interest in *integrating ideas from both* into what could be mutually beneficial in each individual situation. This would require coordination and cooperation on practical and political levels.

The concept of *integration* in the Third agenda represents a *methodological* approach. It means that where the two agendas are used in parallel and, as it often happens, partially overlapping areas there are possibilities for improving their joint activity. Uncoordinated overlapping just doubles the amount of work and does not produce new knowledge or new results. This integration of activities has a large potential for increasing knowledge and capacity and in its most extensive form will lead to full integration. In this case the Third agenda proposes that the methods and tools used by the separate agendas are mutually integrated.

This unity is a public show of strength—an important point in itself. In the case where one organization uses both agendas in its policy and practical work, this unity is already—in ideal situations—established policy-wise within the organizations. Full integration then becomes more of an internal than an external matter. From the general public's perspective it becomes one organization making one statement. Its weight and impact comes from that single organization's weight.

But there are also options in cases where full integration is not used. On the basis of mutual respect for each other's qualities, the two agendas have much to gain from identifying a common working space through partial integration. In this case, *integration* means adjusting one's own position. This does not mean giving one's view, but relating it—for instance of what needs to be assessed and what can be left aside—to a set of other priorities.

In the case of separate organizations working from Human Rights and Peace-Building agendas, respectively, project-orientated integration becomes a method of showing unity on critical points. Such examples could be a demand for an end to capital punishment, the promotion of rights and working conditions for journalists, educational youth work and seminars, training in human rights and peace, etc. Another example is a community's accompaniment of a democratically elected person exposed to threats or accompanying children exposed to a military occupation as a demonstration of concrete presence in support of the right to life against those that formulate the threat. In the same way that human rights may mean protection from threats in a physical sense, peace-building may mean building a school or a house for a health worker together with people from the former enemy group. There is a long list of such mutually uncontroversial positions and demands, illustrated through such projects.

Now, the question naturally arises: why integrate partial or whole agendas if they are not planning to work together? Does integration not first require an agreement to work together? The answer is both "yes" and "no." It has a value in itself, for instance, for a peace-building organization to be informed about what is happening and for them to take into account perspectives and approaches developed by a human rights organization, and vice versa—even if one of them does not have a project idea in common in the foreseeable future. The possibility for such a project to develop may actually increase under such circumstances.

Twinning—Preparing the Way for Each Other

Twinning means that one agenda uses new and recently created space for social, economic, or political action—space that is created by the other agenda. One agenda is then making way for the other, to put it simply. If coordinated this makes up a strategy for mutual reinforcement of the two agendas. As with *integration*, this is a strategy that holds for separate organizations as well as for desks or departments within one single organization.

From post-conflict periods, we know, for instance, about situations where the launching of concrete and specific human rights-based demands can unify a recently liberated population—for achieving fundamental rights or long-term justice-building. Also the opposite may happen: some human rights-based demands can work divisively and reactivate old conflict patterns, and some peace-building activities may be needed initially to form the necessary community strength to deal with such demands.

Let us take as an example a country with high levels political tension and polarization, which present high risks for NGOs in their work. If a human rights organization has to work and express itself on a general and seemingly non-threatening level due to political risks, a peace-building organization can in the same environment take a single, small, and concrete initiative —unthreatening due to its limitations—to illustrate what peace-building in this context can be. However, the two initiatives can go together very well in a planned way: the peace-building initiative is an illustration of how human rights can be realized. If so, the two initiatives are twinned in order to create new space for action by the two involved organizations by combining and using the public awareness that is created in each example.

Sometimes a human rights call for strengthened rights implementation by a government can unify and bridge tension in a community. It brings a sense of coherence and togetherness to make unified claims. If this effect is achieved, further peace-building and dialogue is possibly based on this and therefore provides a continuing possibility for addressing other communal issues.

Also the opposite development may happen: human rights demands, even for fundamental human rights, for victims can bring back old tensions and conflicts. Therefore peace-building through dialogue and identification of a common ground can—under such circumstances—be a more effective road to pave the way for (forthcoming) claims for justice through human rights. When common ground is then established, human rights demands may not cause splits in the same way as it might without the preceding peace-building.

FIGURE 13: Twinning

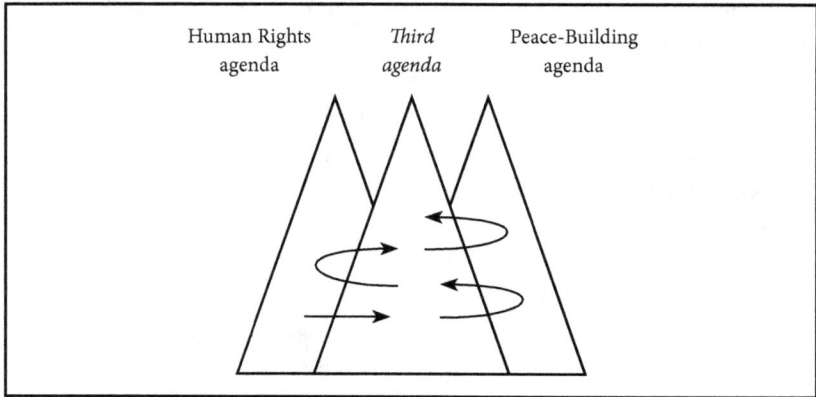

Through a strategic initiative of this kind, it is possible to multiply the strength of the two agendas on local levels in a way that would not be possible if the coordination was not undertaken. It means putting one's own agenda—or one's own agenda-specific department in an organization—in a strategic relationship with another agenda. There is a risk for misunderstanding here: one agenda may think that one has to "wait for the other." However, this can never happen, since it is the new political or social space created by one agenda that is used by the other. To "wait" means not implementing what is already possible. *Twinning* means implementing things that would not have been possible without the other agenda's (successful) action.

Summarizing the Three Components of the Third Agenda

In short, the three approaches in the Third agenda are operating in different ways. While the *common assumption* approach is a matter of principle, guiding the policy foundation of a specific project or program, *integration* is a practical method that constructs a specific design of a project or program. *Twinning*, finally, is a matter of coordinating activities that in themselves are not changed or adapted for crossing agenda borders.

CONCEPTS FOR CHANGE

For the concrete realization of the Third agenda we introduce concepts that develop a specific and mutual understanding of how to combine the Peace-Building and Human Rights agendas. Obviously these concepts cannot be more than illustrations of possibilities. To emphasize the interplay through tactical measures in order to develop joint concrete and short-term approaches we introduce a set of new concepts. This is done in order to show the possibilities through the three methodological approaches.

During the *conflict phase*, which is developed in detail below, three *concepts for change* are introduced to illustrate the specific nature of the Third agenda: *interdependent analysis, giving hope*, and *preparing change*. In addition a fourth concept will be mentioned here, namely *special measures*.

Of all the activities indicated above and initiated in this phase, the conflict phase aims at establishing conditions for a peace commitment. The peace commitment is here considered as a turning point, changing the process from a conflict phase into a post-conflict phase. This is a basis for the promotion of the Third agenda and creates space for initiatives that otherwise would not be possible to realize, since they build upon features of the first two agendas. From an implementation point of view, this will serve as a basis for the post-conflict phase.

During the *post-conflict phase*, the new concepts introduced are *improving economic and social conditions, back to the truth*, and *establishing transitional mechanisms*. The post-conflict phase is to be considered as a transitional period serving as a temporary mechanism. The activities strengthened through the promotion of the Third agenda aim at creating a situation whereby the rule of law is established. Based on the rule of law, it is possible to enter into the next phase—stabilization. The *stabilization phase*, still with a time limit, ends when the state is able to fulfill its functions, leaving the past behind and directed to the future. In this phase we use the concepts of *establishing norms, building institutions*, and *experiencing trust*.

In summary, the concepts for change during the different phases can be seen in Figure 14 below.

FIGURE 14: Concepts for Change to be Used During Phases in Focus

1. CONFLICT PHASE			
ONGOING VIOLENCE AND WAR		OCCUPATION	GENOCIDE
Making an Inter-dependent Analysis	Giving Hope	Preparing Change	Special Measures
Peace Commitment			
2. POST-CONFLICT PHASE			
TRANSFORMATION			
Improving Economic and Social Conditions	Coming Back to the Truth		Establishing Transitional Mechanisms
Rule of Law			
3. STABILIZATION PHASE			
TOWARDS NORMALIZATION			
Establishing Norms	Building Institutions		Experiencing Trust

5

The Third Agenda during a Conflict Phase

THIS CHAPTER DEALS WITH the first of the three phases—the conflict phase. We will illustrate how the three methodological approaches of the Third agenda (*common assumption, integration* and *twinning*) can be understood and implemented by building on four concepts of change in this particular phase. These concepts are: *interdependent analysis, giving hope, preparing change*, and *special measures*.

MAKING USE OF THE METHODOLOGICAL APPROACH OF COMMON ASSUMPTION

A fundamental way to address the matter would be to apply an overarching principle recognized—and used—by both sides in this discussion, namely the principle of "the right to life." It should serve, we propose, as a *guiding principle for action that is possible to justify in situations of friction.* Instead of allowing the friction to stall or make ineffective a progress towards an end of violence and a new development, a more holistic assessment of the situation, based on the right to life as a principle, should be made. If more lives are likely to be spared, in a given situation, by including human rights issues in this process, this should be done. If more lives are likely to be spared, in a given situation, by focusing on ending ongoing violence rather than pursuing human rights demands at that point in time, this should be done. In either of the two situations, the process is incomplete: human rights principles do not implement themselves, even if included, and an end to violence does not in itself protect any right besides the right to life. The main point is to overcome the point of friction between the agendas by a principled approach.

MAKING USE OF THE METHODOLOGICAL
APPROACH OF INTEGRATION

To use *integration* as a methodological approach means to depart from the idea that the Peace-Building and Human Rights agendas, when taken separately, have components that are relevant *for the other* agenda. In this case the Third agenda proposes that the separate agendas are fully integrated, partially integrated, or at least used in a project-oriented integration. Such a methodological approach is necessary to achieve long-term commitments and projects. The concepts for change in the conflict phase—*interdependent analysis, giving hope, preparing change,* and *special measures*—are the activities that, taken together, may indicate full integration, used in some part to indicate a partial integration or taken selectively end up in a project-oriented integration. We should admit that the borderline is sometimes fine between what we identify as *giving hope* and *preparing change*; it is a matter of emphasis.

This means that when the connection between "principle and action" is made visible, there is an obvious incentive that promotes change. The link between the two perspectives creates a critical mass within the integration of the Third agenda.

We will begin, below, with the example of the content in an *interdependent analysis* as a means towards full integration.

Interdependent Analysis

The purpose of an *interdependent analysis* here is to construct a comprehensive understanding of a conflict setting, based on insights from both agendas. Dimensions that normally are identified only by one agenda, actually may contribute substantially to the understanding of the content of the other agenda. The analysis can be structured and written in different ways, but in terms of content the following points seem to be a necessary starting point:

- *history* (uncontested basic facts; issues from the history of each party that today are the basis for pursuing one's goals);

- *context* (present conditions for the conflict);

- identify *human rights instruments* and *International Humanitarian Law*;

- identify the *conflict parties* (primary and secondary parties);

- identify the *duty bearers*;
- describe the *issues* that the (primary and secondary) parties fight for;
- identify the directly exposed *rights holders*;
- identify *gender* dimensions of power and social structures;
- describe the conflict's *dynamics*—escalation/de-escalation phases;
- identify humanitarian and social *consequences* (Who are victims? Women? Children? Elderly?);
- identify the *conflict-formed actors*, both as a complicating factor and possible resource, for the local and international civil society;
- identify vulnerable and excluded *groups* as targeted groups, refugees, and internally displaced people;
- *settlement proposals/mediation attempts* during the conflict process (under human rights and International Humanitarian Law instruments can a peace process take place?).

While it may be obvious how the various dimensions mentioned in this list mutually reinforce each other, below we will develop examples of this by commenting on a few of the points.

ANALYSIS OF HISTORY AND CONTEXT

In many conflicts history plays an important role, even if interpreted through the present conditions. For an *interdependent analysis* it is important to identify those aspects that are based on *historic* conditions, including issues and claims made on this basis. This means that when the parties specifically refer to historic events or conditions as a basis for demands in today's conflict, this has to be included in the interdependent analysis. The question is sometimes if history provides more than moral arguments for a position. Is there a legal aspect of historically founded claims? In particular in land rights issues, the legal dimension of historic events and practice is closely connected to the interpretation of today's conflict and its potential settlement.

While history has its place, in any violent conflict situation it is also necessary, as early as possible, to get an adequate understanding of the conflict context. *Context* means all those conditions under which the present conflict takes place. It refers to everything from major structural conditions (such as rich/poor country, mountainous or not, climate, a history of wars, international commitments, administration, infrastructure, literacy and health status) to specific features of specific areas (language/ethnic diversity, HIV, drug cultivation, etc.). The context embraces the conflict and defines the sociopolitical and physical "landscape" for the conflict, its parties and its consequences.

The purpose of an analysis beginning with history and context is—in principle—to provide both donors and parties a picture that contains an all-round and balanced picture of critical positions and facts in the conflict.

Identifying Relevant Human Rights Instruments and International Humanitarian Law

Closely connected to the contextual analysis is one area that needs special attention, namely the legal situation. In a military conflict the national law, International Humanitarian Law, and human rights instruments exist as norms for what is allowed to be done in a war and how to treat the civil population. These regulations are not automatically applicable in every situation since the state/states involved must have ratified the agreements before being culpable for applying the obligations. The International Humanitarian Law is a set of conventions promoted and guarded by the International Committee of the Red Cross. The human rights instruments are of course the main covenants from the UN but can also include regional agreements like the African (Banjul) Charter on Human and Peoples' Rights, the American Convention on Human Rights, and the European Convention on Human Rights and Fundamental Freedoms.

In an interdependent analysis it is important to figure out which regulations are applicable in general and what specific articles can be used to urge fighting parties to reduce direct violations and protect the civil population.

Identifying the Conflict Parties, Victims, Rights Holders, and Duty Bearers

Using the language from the human rights–based approach and from peace-building will further clarify the relation between a matrix of parties, groups, segments of the population, and individuals, thus clarifying whose rights are being violated, who are the perpetrators and who are responsible for conducting violations.

Parties, their supporters, as well as victims from the conflict are critical parts of an interdependent analysis. In a way, parties constitute what is often perceived as "the conflict." Without parties there can be no conflict. The parties can be two governments (in an international conflict) or a government and one or more opposition/rebel groups (in a civil war). Obviously, the parties are often dependent on support from inside or outside their country. All violent and militarized parties sooner or later become a direct or indirect threat to the civil population, which then becomes involved either in a supportive role or not. A conflict situation in this way forces different groups and individuals into an initial position as victims (since they were forcefully exposed to unwanted changes), something that is dealt with and sometimes changed by themselves and/or national and international initiatives. To be able to leave victimhood behind and become an actor is then an important factor for change.

In an ongoing violent conflict a focus on the rights holders and especially on the most marginalized and discriminated against in a society is vital. In this part of the analysis, the rights holders, according to human rights instruments and International Humanitarian Law, are in focus. In the same way as identifying rights holders, there is a need to map who the duty bearers are and, as a consequence, what their obligations are and what violations they may be performing. In this way it does not matter whether the perpetrator is a state, a rebel group, or any other type of non-state actor—it is always about the protection of the individual against abuse. At the same time, mapping human rights violations gives a clear indication about the causes of a particular conflict.

The following points need to be dealt with by all of the categories: *parties* (mainly state/states and groups active in a conflict), *victims* (mainly individuals/groups suffering from a conflict), *rights holders* (mainly individuals as legal entities with legal rights), and *duty bearers* (mainly state bodies as legal entities with legal duties):

- who they are;
- how they present themselves in relation to the conflict;
- what their situation is; (newly formed or old);

- what their strengths and weaknesses are;
- what are possible needs for development;
- what their rights and entitlements are and, in applicable cases, what their duties are;
- what formal and informal structures (laws, policies, rules, etc.) they relate to;
- how they relate with each other and with formal and informal structures;
- which capacities need to be strengthened.

Concerning *rights holders* and *victims* the following points should also be addressed:

- applicable rights even if the person is not yet aware of them;
- their capacities, as individual members of society and perhaps as members of formal or informal organized entities in society.

Finally, for *parties* and *duty bearers* the following points are also relevant:

- their ideologies and interests;
- value systems governing their actions;
- their obligations—whether they are immediate or progressive (or both)—and the levels of these obligations;
- their capacities, military and civilian.

IDENTIFYING NEW VULNERABLE AND EXCLUDED GROUPS

In a conflict situation, persons belonging to groups that have been characterized as vulnerable before the conflict may be even more so and become particularly targeted throughout the conflict. Among the marginalized are often minority groups possibly based on ethnicity, religion, language, etc. In several conflicts these kinds of minority characteristics are also part of the cause of the conflict, which brings the group into a situation of being directly targeted, as in Rwanda or the eastern part of the Congo.

There are also new vulnerable groups appearing as a consequence of war and violence. Refugees and internally displaced people are examples of this: many of them have already been exposed to violence, have had their basic livelihoods destroyed, and are trying to escape direct violence.

One consequence of war is that women and children are particularly exposed. Special attention must be paid to child soldiers, who can be forced or bribed to be direct participants in fighting forces. Thereby they become both victims and a possible perpetrators in a conflict. Concerning the rights holders, it is important to monitor and evaluate who they are and, as a consequence, investigate what their situation is and what their rights and entitlements are.

IDENTIFYING THE CONFLICT-FORMED ACTORS

With the inclusion of the conflict-formed actors a more profound understanding of the situation is possible. Thus, the civil population—which is not part of the parties, victims, duty bearers, or rights holders—will be included in the analysis to the extent that it adapts to the new conditions created by the conflict. For this category, the following points need to be addressed:

- how they present themselves;
- their management of the situation, such as adaption—i.e., changed work and life conditions—to the conflict or resisting its consequences;
- what their capacities are as individuals and as members of organized entities (including sub-organizational units);
- preferences on returning, e.g., to pre-conflict conditions or remaining in their present location;
- value systems governing their activities;
- formal and informal structures (laws, policies, rules, etc.) they operate within;
- how they relate with each other—if at all;
- how they relate with formal and informal social structures (such as the civil society).

In this way, individuals and groups who, because of the conflict, adjust or change their life and work profoundly, become included in the analysis. While normally easily overlooked in analyses, their inclusion could be useful in a process towards ending the conflict as well.

Identifying Humanitarian and Social Consequences

A situation where people suffer in an indiscriminate and unpredictable way comes close to the core elements of a *humanitarian* crisis. This is a situation that challenges fundamental life conditions, and it becomes internationally relevant when national resources are not capable of dealing with the situation or neglect to do so for some reason.

Social consequences are a wider issue and of another nature. They are often not directly life-threatening. In a short-term perspective they are more difficult to trace and indicate, even if some affects are obvious and well known from previous or similar situations. A long-term perspective is often needed for identifying their nature and effects in a society. Nevertheless, it is the social consequences that in the long-term will constitute the reasons for an international NGO to work in post-conflict societies. To make a first estimate of their nature and scope therefore makes sense.

Without a full consideration of these perspectives in an early analysis—i.e., in the interdependent analysis—the humanitarian and social consequences will be secondary as a background variable for deciding on human rights or peace-building efforts. If a local situation is characterized by its humanitarian dimensions more than anything else, this is an obvious aspect that needs to be included in the analytical framework as early as possible.

Issues, Dynamics, and Settlement Attempts

A conflict is often described by its many manifestations: besides killing, bombing, and general destruction is hatred, prejudice, and anger. All of them are "media-prone" and therefore they tend to shape our image of a conflict. However, without contested issues there is no conflict—parties have goals, and when these clash with other parties' goals the result is conflict. To identify what the parties actually are fighting for is a basic tool for coming to grips with the dynamics and possible settlement of a conflict.

The information from this part of the analysis lies as a foundation for ideas and proposals for a settlement—both in terms of process and content. Without a solid issue analysis, finding common ground for conflict resolution cannot be expected. Having recognized this, we also need to recognize that problems and claims are both changing throughout a conflict process. Additionally, new issues—not the least as a consequence of violations of human rights—come up and need to be dealt with in order to end a conflict.

For the interdependent analysis as a whole, the issue and settlement dimension is the most dynamic one, since this is when the conflict changes its perspective "from history to future."

Giving Hope

The purpose of the concept *giving hope* is to produce concrete evidence that peace, human rights and development are possible when a conflict has ended. In a situation of war and violent conflict, as well as during occupation, giving hope means turning the theoretical concepts of "human rights" and "peace" into actions for change. Since we are in the *conflict phase*, this means actions that put an end to ongoing violations and push the parties towards a *peace commitment*. We realize that giving hope may sound like a slogan more than a plan for action, but a number of measures can be taken and used as pressure upon the parties:

- monitoring state and non-state actors (with special attention to torture, extra-judicial killings, disappearances, arbitrary detention, abductions and unfair trials);

- bringing to light direct violations against human rights and International Humanitarian Law in connection to war/occupation;

- efforts to get an end to ongoing violence;

- trust-building within the civil society (for instance through information sharing);

- trust-building between conflicting parties (facilitating dialogue, negotiation and support from civil society for the process);

- approaching conflict-formed actors (such as farmers, homeless people, refugees or displaced persons, individually or organized as NGOs);

- building trust mechanisms (civil society based relations on all sides, for instance in monitoring, verification, and bridging security dilemma situations).

We will now comment on these dimensions following the pattern of the previous section.

Monitoring and Disclosing Patterns of Human Rights Abuses

In giving hope, as in many other situations, monitoring violations of human rights is a necessary step. In a conflict phase it is vital to claim simultaneously the importance of all human rights, including both civil and political rights, and economic, social, and cultural rights. In a situation of war or open violence, the human rights are still applicable in all their aspects. This said, in special situations there is a need of putting special emphasis on specific aspects of the human rights system. Priorities can be given on practical grounds. In a situation of violent conflict or war, the strategies concerning human rights are focused on a process of keeping respect for and protection of fundamental political and civil rights.

TABLE 3: Stressing Certain Human Rights During a Conflict Situation*

	Respect (no interference in the exercise of the right)	**Protect** (prevent violations from third parties)	**Fulfill** (provision of resources and the outcomes of policies)
Civil and Political rights	*Measures to prevent state actors from committing torture, extra-judicial killings, disappearances, arbitrary detention, unfair trials, electoral intimidation, and disenfranchisement.*	*Measures to prevent non-state actors from committing violations, such as torture, extra-judicial killings, disappearances, abduction, and electoral intimidation.*	Investment in judiciaries, prisons, police forces, elections, and resource allocations commensurate with ability.
Economic, Social, and Cultural rights	Measures to prevent state actors from committing ethnic, racial, gender or linguistic discrimination in health, education and welfare, and resource allocations below ability.	Measures to prevent non-state actors from engaging in discriminatory behavior that limits access to health, education, and other welfare provisions.	Progressive realization. Investment in health, education and welfare, and resource allocations commensurate with ability.

* Measures specially discussed in this section in italics.

In a situation of war, the civil society, if at all able to function, is challenged to monitor and analyze to what extent the state is responsible for committing violations of its human rights obligations (respect) as well as being able to prevent non-state parties from violating human rights (protect). It is specifically important to monitor and evaluate to what extent violations are taking place, such as torture, extra-judicial killings, arbitrary detention, unfair trials, and disappearances.

Bringing to Light Direct Violations in Connection to War

In a situation of war, as well as under occupation, a new set of laws enters into force through "the laws of war"—the International Humanitarian Law—in order to limit the affects of armed international and non-international conflicts and to protect those not involved as direct combatants, such as the civil population, the wounded, sick, and prisoners of war. The International Humanitarian Law at the same time restricts both the means and the methods of warfare.

TABLE 4: Respect and Protection According to International Humanitarian Law

	Respect and Protect (all parties in relation to non-combatants)
International as well as non-international conflict	Prohibiting murder, mutilation, torture, cruel treatment, the taking of hostages, and outrages upon personal dignity, in particular humiliating and degrading treatment. Protect lives, moral and physical integrity, personal rights and convictions, treating humanely without any adverse distinction, respect fundamental judicial guarantees, prohibit forbidden methods and means of warfare*, respect the emblem of the Red Cross and the Red Crescent. * With respect to forbidden methods and means of warfare there may be a difference between international and non-international conflict, due to different interpretations of customary law.

The monitoring of "war abuses" (like torture, extra-judicial killings, taking of hostages, cruel treatment, disappearances, arbitrary detentions, and unfair trials) will focus on giving the rights holders a message that this is not acceptable and at the same time show the duty-bearing parties their responsibilities as well as the possibilities to protect actual and potential victims.

This process of monitoring both human rights and humanitarian laws needs, if at all possible pursue, to involve the rights holders themselves since they, as those being targeted and whose rights are being violated, are the ones holding the relevant information. In this monitoring process it may be necessary to involve international organizations with their resources for assistance.

EFFORTS TO REACH AN END TO ONGOING VIOLENCE

The concepts used—the "language," so to speak—are primarily examples and encouragement for action, not claims vis-à-vis the duty bearer, since there is an urgent need to attain an end to ongoing violence. It is the open and direct forms of violence, including killing, that are in focus here. This violence is not only the expression of war and armed conflict, it also makes relief impossible and prevents important elements of society from functioning, such as hospitals, schools, and food distribution. Finally, it kills soldiers and civilians, including children, the elderly, women, and men. Giving hope is in this context pointing at the need for creating a sign of possibilities, possibilities that lie in the long-term execution of a project, initiative, or program.

It is not an exaggeration to claim that all major conflicts—in particular protracted conflicts—have many "cracks in the wall" of manifested unity: there are initiatives to break cycles of escalation (Timor-Leste), villages that resist being involved (Philippines), local initiatives for reconciliation (Colombia), dialogue centers that create bridges (Middle East, Northern Ireland), and other examples that all need to be brought forward and strengthened in various ways, or as much as is possible in their often precarious working conditions. This option supports the trust-building function, since trust is a common denominator between the agendas.

TRUST-BUILDING

It is probably a truism to say that a vibrant society has a component of both trust and rights. This implies that there are both duty bearers and rights holders. In a human rights perspective, it is the individual that is the rights holder, and (normally) it is the state that is a duty bearer. In a trust-based peace-building perspective, it is the individual that is the duty bearer (trust is an attitude we take in the service of others) and the society that is the rights holder (our neighbors have the right to be trusted and not suspected without reason).

In order to attain this, a number of issues need to already be settled during the conflict phase. Parties with some sort of power may otherwise not allow disarmament if they do not know what they face. For instance, many guerrilla leaders may prefer an ordered legal procedure to an uncertain civil life, with its risks of all kinds of threats from former and current enemies. The sticking point is the word "ordered." The questions are: What will happen afterwards? Who can secure what will happen to me/us, if our arms are given up? The *security dilemma* illustrates this way of thinking: if one side gives up, who makes sure that the other side is not cheating and afterwards brings out their hidden weapons? This is particularly serious for movements in conflict with the state, which has a legitimate right to use of force/arms, and therefore cannot be demobilized—how is a state, which may have recently been violating fundamental human rights, controlled so that this will not happen again?

Obviously, building trust between populations living under different rulers/identities, such as in Congo (DRC), the Middle East, or Timor-Leste, will reduce the risk for populism and hatred. In particular, international NGOs have a possibility in national and local settings to function as connectors[1] between groups and organizations, and can open closed attitudes that other actors would "never" be able to change.

Approaching Conflict-formed Actors

Some conflict-formed actors, such as farmers with devastated land, people made homeless as a result of direct fighting, refugees and displaced people, have immediate needs. These rights holders' situations—as individuals, entire villages, and organized as NGOs—need to be addressed if giving hope is to be effective. Their immediate situation—shelter, food and water, and basic security—as well as a more long-term hope of a new and normal life situation, are components in such a process of giving hope.

---

1. "Connector" in the sense of Mary B. Anderson's "Do No Harm" terminology, i.e., someone who on the basis of common interests (all groups have *some* common interests, according to Anderson) brings together groups that normally would consider the other group as a (total) enemy.

Without being too prejudiced, it may be observed here that conflict-formed actors—through their very existence—may not be able to contribute by their own strength to giving hope, instead many of them have found a way of life based on and adapted to the conditions formed by the conflict. For this reason, the international or national civil society may need to specifically address these groups in order to bring them into a role that is constructive for change. This is further developed below.

BUILDING TRUST MECHANISMS

Here we take the step from *trust-building* to establishing *trust mechanisms*. Even in situations where there is a degree of trust between the parties, this is not sufficient to secure against cheating, as described above. Therefore a third-party mechanism that can verify promises and actions is a critical instrument. Such mechanisms are often considered a state responsibility, or something for the international community to take care of. However, it happens now and then that the civil society—perhaps through the Red Cross/Crescent, national church organizations, or local NGOs—takes care of monitoring as well as the construction of multi-party mechanisms to eliminate security dilemmas. A case in point is the Philippines, where local NGOs have been monitoring a cease-fire and demobilization. This has also been contemplated in other conflict areas in the world. As long as all parties concerned are involved, the risk for being considered biased—something many civil society organizations are afraid of—is indeed very low. This should, of course, be a categorical condition since it is for the good of all, not just some, that such a mechanism is neutral and effective.

Preparing Change

The conflict phase is characterized by destruction, defensiveness, and limitations of resources. Because of this, it is necessary not only for local communities but also for the surrounding national and international communities—which themselves are often represented in the conflict zones—to show the possibilities that are always there if peace and human rights are to be established.

Preparing for change has two components. One component means to assess the affects of monitoring, of opinion-building and ongoing capacity-building carried out under the previous concepts in this phase (such as evaluating ongoing monitoring of abuses), so as to make sure that there is a normative and democratic capacity among all affected groups to initiate a new social life the day when the violent phase of the conflict ends (and we go into the post-conflict phase). Another component is to create incentives for this preparedness to change into a state of permanent cease-fire and, in the longer perspective, a nonviolent political life and peace. In the same way conflict and war are almost synonymous with destruction, peace should be visible and synonymous with construction. How can this be illustrated? The sticking point is the time-lag between words and deeds: if there is change towards peace among the parties, this should be positively responded to by the civil society. One party's change should be reciprocated by the other party—this should be a strong claim by the civil society. The construction of a "benign circle"—a mutually reinforcing development of constructive ideas and practices—is something that the civil society can both claim, contribute to, and partially realize itself. For instance, this can be made by taking the risks of crossing a social or physical boundary, of talking to the other side, or of building the capacity to administer change.

How can change be prepared? Preparing change includes, as far as possible during a conflict phase, these points:

- opinion-building—locally, nationally and internationally—in order for "naming and shaming";

- initiatives that demonstrate certain tangible improvements (joint actions in public areas; "small" initiatives in the midst of harsh conditions make a difference: road repair for hospital access, making ambulances available, school repairs, etc.);

- activities linked to a peace-process (stopping hostage taking means starting dialogue, and progressing dialogue means development projects);

- disclosing patterns of human rights abuses;

- humanitarian corridors (for vaccinations and other humanitarian assistance).

DISCLOSING PATTERNS OF HUMAN RIGHTS ABUSES

The monitoring process is, in one way, an event-based data collection. Numerical summaries and rights holder's descriptive stories tell about when and what has happened, to whom and by whom. Patterns are disclosed and reported, and what might initially seem to be occasional cases can, taken together, indicate a more systematic degree of violation. During the phase of direct conflict the deliberate targeting of civilians can result in homelessness, displacement, etc. The special civil and political rights endangered in a war situation are also on the agenda.

OPINION-BUILDING

The monitoring is a base for opinion-building locally, nationally, and internationally through media, institutions, international organizations, councils, and governments. The affect of "shaming" is of importance, especially since governments in war, as well as "war lords," are aware of possible national or international tribunals after a war. The monitoring also gives a starting point for decisions about humanitarian needs and assistance for the remaining local civilian population as well as refugees and displaced people.

In direct war situations it is not easy to strengthen the capacity of either duty bearers or rights holders. Still it is important to work actively in the field and not least in order to, as early as possible, build up awareness among refugees and displaced people about their rights, thus creating a readiness to enter into a post-conflict phase.

The timing for opinion-building is essential for at least some of the *conflict-formed actors* to be involved in and informed about what is happening. Their involvement must be coordinated with other steps taken in the process. These groups will now have a new role to play in this phase if they want to contribute to their society's development.

SUPPORTING VISIBLE IMPROVEMENTS

Initiating preparations for making studies, providing financing, facilitating pick-up idea sessions, as well as capacity-building and advocacy for parties, duty bearers, rights holders, and conflict-formed actors, are made in order to be as prepared as possible the day peace comes. This will imply the need to initiate preparations for reconstruction already in this phase. Yet it does not mean that one is overlooking immediate humanitarian concerns, but in order to avoid stagnation of hearts and minds in a victim-helper perspective, it is critical that possibilities and prospects for a soon-coming better future are made realistic with the help of all sides.

ACTIVITIES LINKED TO A PEACE PROCESS

To be able to link a peace commitment with tangible improvements makes the commitment much more credible. The lack of this condition has been clearly visible, for instance, in the Congo (DRC) after the Lusaka Agreement, where there was a lot of hesitation internationally to support after the agreement was signed. In Timor-Leste this has been a major challenge after independence. In Colombia there is no national vision of a "country without war." Politics, meaning the public debates on ideology and economy, are ingrained by the national conflict. In Guatemala there was never a binding commitment in the peace agreement to making improvements, and the civil society is struggling with the legacy of what was once a national, deep-running peace process. Today they are trying to make the best of a beautiful peace agreement text.

ESTABLISHING HUMANITARIAN CORRIDORS

One result of an ongoing conflict is the creation of conflict-formed actors. In most conflicts it is the women and children that suffer the most. With homes destroyed, possibilities for getting daily food and water limited, and widespread insecurity, people are driven into refugee situations hiding out in the countryside or in destroyed cities and villages. For those people survival is a question of receiving external help. This also goes for people hurt by natural catastrophes, such as earthquakes and tornado. Establishing a humanitarian corridor enabling basic resources for the population is a necessity for survival and a sign of preparing change in a hopeless situation.

Special Measures

When a violent conflict escalates into severe crimes during a war, special measures must be taken. These are established as international commitments when the violence has passed the limit for respecting the principle of non-intervention and has turned, for instance, into cruelties such as crimes against humanity, war crimes, genocide, or ethnic cleansing. In *special measures* we include the *responsibility to protect* (often shortened to R2P), humanitarian or military interventions, or other forms of so-called collective defense measures.[2] NGOs do not actively commit

2. This refers to the discussion on the development of international customary law, for instance in relation to the question of NATO and Kosovo.

themselves on a regular basis to initiate and/or implement these kinds of measures. Some are, however, important not to give up even in the gravest of situations:

- monitoring and disseminating developments and human rights violations;

- demonstrating the consequences (for instance environmental) of the violence;

- establishing international resources in order to deal with the aftermath of the conflict.

WHEN A WAR TRESPASSES INTO THE MOST SERIOUS CRIMES

The monitoring and evaluation during the conflict phase of open violence needs to disclose severe violations of human rights and at the same time evaluate if the borderline has been passed transforming the conflict into war crimes.

TABLE 5: Respect and Protection When War Is Escalating into War Crimes

	Respect (no interference in the exercise of the right)	**Protect** (prevent violations from third parties)
Civil and Political rights	Measures to prevent state actors from committing torture, extra-judicial killings, disappearances, arbitrary detention, unfair trials, electoral intimidation, and disenfranchisement.	Measures to prevent non-state actors from committing violations, such as torture, extra-judicial killings, disappearances, abduction, and electoral intimidation.

Measures taken against:

Genocide
Crimes against humanity
War crimes
Crime of aggression

In violent crises or ongoing wars, it is not unusual that the part believing their civil population is exposed to killings or threats urge the international community to intervene to end human rights violations and crimes against International Humanitarian Law. Military force or use of military means in a serious humanitarian crisis must be based on a mandate of the UN Security Council. Diana Amnéus has raised the question of whether there may exist a responsibility to protect in other cases, based on regional or other decisions.[3] For example, outside the concept of self-defense, may a collective defense organization, such as NATO, or individual states develop a right (a new customary law) to use military means in special humanitarian crisis situations even without a Security Council resolution? There is no legal basis according to international law legitimizing an individual state or an ad hoc coalition of states to intervene with military means even if they want to take on the responsibility of providing protection in an ongoing humanitarian crisis or other severe violations of human rights such as genocide or crimes against humanity.

The rules for military interventions have been referred to partially above. It is interesting to note that this final expression of the right to collective defense laid out in the UN Charter, is referred to also in both R2P and humanitarian intervention documents. The classical theme of a people's right to topple a tyrant is here finding its modern expression.

REVEALING MECHANISMS OF OCCUPATION

The rules concerning an occupation differ from those pertaining to human rights—usually being individual rights. True, there are regulations concerning individuals but also about what is and in not allowed to be done in the occupied territories.

---

3. See Amnéus, *Responsibility to Protect.*

TABLE 6: Protection During Occupation

	Duties (occupying power in relation to civil population and occupied territory)
Occupation	<ul><li>not acquire sovereignty over the territory</li><li>ensure sufficient hygiene and public health standards</li><li>the provision of food and medical care</li><li>measures to restore and ensure, as far as possible, public order and safety</li><li>transfers of population from and within the occupied territory are prohibited</li><li>collective punishment is prohibited</li><li>taking of hostages is prohibited</li><li>confiscation of private property is prohibited</li><li>destruction or seizure of enemy property</li><li>proceedings respecting internationally recognized judicial guarantees for persons accused of criminal offences</li></ul>

HUMANITARIAN INTERVENTION/MILITARY INTERVENTION

The principle of non-intervention is one of the cornerstones in the international state system. If states had the freedom to intervene according to their preferences, no one would be safe or secure from the wills of other states. In practice it would lead to a situations where "might is right." The strongest countries would set the agenda and dictate the solutions.

No one wants this situation to develop, in particular small states who otherwise fear more or less aggressive attitudes from neighboring or bigger states. This principle is also one of the foundations for the UN Charter. The charter makes very clear if and when any deviation from this principle would be acceptable. In brief, it is in chapter 7 of the charter that such conditions are outlined. However, this is in all circumstances a last resort, and other means should be applied first (see Article 33 in the charter).

The typical case of a "clash between principles" is when the respect and protection for human rights fails and the international community of states wants to take action, but is stopped by the host government with reference to the principle of non-intervention. More often than not this government is itself also a violator of human rights.

In order to come around, or find ways to deal with this situation, the concept of a right to humanitarian intervention has been widely discussed among states, international organizations, and not least in the United Nations system. The basic idea is that "states have a responsibility to protect their own citizens from avoiding catastrophe—from mass murder and rape, from starvation—but that when they are unwilling or unable to do so, that responsibility must be borne by the broader community of states."[4] What could constitute a basis for breaking the non-intervention principle? According to one view,[5] it can be any of the following:

- a humanitarian disaster situation;

- a situation of systematic violation of human rights;

- a situation of systematic violation of the principle of justice;

- a situation of systematic violation of the principle of welfare; under the conditions of

- an international Charter-based decision;

- a plan is made for the use of arms only for protection.

Many today consider the UN in the 1990s to have been too ambitious and optimistic regarding the possibility to intervene in situations that challenge fundamental human rights and democracy inside a country, to the extent that it also becomes a threat to international peace and security. A serious critique of this position developed mainly from countries in the South that this ambition was, or could, easily develop into a new colonial mentality from the North. The idea of "humanitarian intervention" was criticized as colonialism in disguise.

Nevertheless, the UN Charter has, since its conception, been the mechanism of collective action against threats to international peace and security. The challenge today is to give this possibility an expression and design that meets the need for integrity with respect for human rights.

The most recent formulation of this collective defense against threats to international peace and security is the concept of a *responsibility to protect* (R2P). A major report on the issue was published in 2001[6]

4. Ibid., VIII.

5. Nordquist, *From "Just War."*

6. Amnéus, *Responsibility to Protect.*

and a Security Council resolution referred to this approach in 2006.[7] The basic idea is that:

> . . . states have a responsibility to protect their own citizens from avoiding catastrophe—from mass murder and rape, from starvation—but that when they are unwilling or unable to do so, that responsibility must be borne by the broader community of states.[8]

The concept is based on a set of standards for a responsibility to protect human rights and international peace and security before intervention (of any sort) should be contemplated.[9] If such measures, or other measures short of military intervention, are not effective there are principles for conditions under which, for instance, the preventive deployment of troops (such as in the case of Macedonia) could take place. As a last resort military intervention may also be contemplated in cases where a host government has—through its actions and policies—consumed all its international credibility and human rights need to be protected from outside. A case in point for this type of reaction is Sudan and the Darfur situation.

To the extent that the R2P concept allows for early initiatives that otherwise would not have been taken without breaking the intervention principle, it is of course for major positive change. However, such measures have been taken and can legitimately be taken on the basis of existing human rights principles.

If an intervention—i.e., a military action against the will of the host country—has to take place, then the difference between R2P and the concept of humanitarian intervention is merely "cosmetic." In both cases it is the protection of humanitarian values that is at stake whether a host government agrees to the international protection efforts or not.

Also in the *military intervention* perspective, as in the case of R2P and humanitarian intervention, there is a clear unanimity between the two agendas on the principles and conditions under which a military intervention is possible to justify.

---

7. On April 28, 2006, the Security Council unanimously adopted Resolution 1674 on the Protection of Civilians in Armed Conflict. The resolution contains the first official Security Council reference to the principle or idea of the responsibility to protect.

8. Amnéus, *Responsibility to Protect*, VIII.

9. See ibid.

MAKING USE OF THE METHODOLOGICAL
APPROACH OF TWINNING

Twinning in this study means "paving way for each other." One agenda takes the first step; the other agenda takes the second step. Together they create a process. This methodological principle can be applied at various operational levels, from individual projects to national programs. For instance, if one agenda's analysis of a situation is made at an early stage of involvement this can function as a preparation for the other agenda's later analysis. Equally, and inside an organization, one agenda-related department can coordinate with another department and create a system of initiatives, or even projects, that create a twinning affect. This can be formulated in spatial terms by saying that the point is to find out how an agenda can use space that another agenda has created but *would not use, since it lies outside that agenda's normal working area.* Thus it never becomes a matter of taking away space for action that an agenda has created, but rather letting someone else utilize the full width of a space that one has created.

Let us look at some possible examples of twinning. It can be constructed in a variety of ways depending on the local conditions. For instance, if respect for fundamental human rights is established, this could in a second step also be a basis for trust-building between parties. The opposite is also possible: if trust has been established between communities, for instance, this may pave the way for a readiness to bring the hard facts of violations of human rights and international humanitarian law into light. One agenda utilizes the space created by the other. Also more complex processes can be envisioned here: based on monitoring and basic trust-building the civil society may call for respect and protection, thereby paving the way for bridging security dilemmas.

Example 1: Justice vs. Peace

If the dilemma behind this study is often called the "justice vs. peace dilemma," it is possible to formulate the same type of relationship between "trust" and "rights." Yet instead of juxtaposing these concepts, one could in the name of twinning apply an approach saying that "trust means rights" and "rights mean trust," arguing that the two should always *build upon* each other. This way of acting creates, for instance, a way to overcome the focus on the individual level that characterizes the Human

Rights agenda, as well as the group orientation that often characterizes a Peace-Building agenda.

Is there reason to believe that this is more than a theoretical speculation? Probably. When trust is established on a most fundamental level—for instance for a legal system—even if only rudimentary in its form, it is also possible to bring to light and deal with violations through ad hoc mechanisms or through that legal system. Violations are commonplace, and probably carried out by many or all sides in a conflict. In order to deal with this, some fundamental trust is required—a trust that may not be in the parties' willingness to come forward, but at least in the legal system and its legitimacy (often lacking after an internal conflict). When such trust is established, the system can start functioning. A next level of trust-building in a society requires more elaborate mechanisms and forms of human rights defense. There is trust developed over time as an expression of acceptance in the actions of the system itself. A new level of trust is reached.

In this way, building trust makes way for defending rights. And defending rights creates new levels of trust. A benign circle is established and both the agendas and the post-conflict society will benefit from such a process.

Example 2: Polarization

To give another situation where twinning can be an effective methodological approach, we will investigate two aspects of social polarization. In both cases twinning can be useful.

It is, for instance, possible to argue that twinning can be effective in a *politically highly polarized* situation. In some conflict situations, such as in the Middle East, Colombia, Sri Lanka, and other protracted conflict situations, the polarization between groups in the society is so high that problems that in other societies would be regarded as more or less technical become serious and quickly can turn into high-level political issues. Drawing maps, and naming places or streets, building or houses are examples that come close to politically sensitive issues.

It is probably true that *the more polarized a society is the more important is an analysis based on non-party-related dimensions*, such as international human rights standards. A human rights–based analysis is established on a normative framework that is different from the polarized political agendas in the society. Thus a human rights–based approach could introduce perspectives that otherwise would not have been accepted as issues for public discussion in that country. Dimensions in such a human rights–based analysis should be as few as possible—in order not to interfere with the polarized agendas at this stage—using, for instance, only the triangle of violations, rights holders, and duty bearers in a focused and neutral way.

As a second step—and here begins the twinning—when an acceptance of these issues has been made it is then possible to introduce a peace-building approach, starting with an analysis of conflict and conflict resolution possibilities, which may introduce a variety of approaches, including different actors with different approaches and ways and means by which they all could do something about it. This form of twinning, again, works because a third, normative perspective is introduced beside the polarized political perspectives. The more different from a political language the human rights–based approach is, the more possible it is to use in polarized situations.

Let us reflect on a situation that is opposite to the polarized one, where the twinning approach might also work if initiated from a peace-building perspective. Let us consider a society that is highly divided among competing local traditions, be they cultural, ethnic, religious, or other forms of agendas. To introduce yet another normative system—the human rights system—is more likely to be possible if such an introduction is preceded by a politically developed, joint platform of simple rules for dialogue between the traditions. To initiate such a process is a typical common ground–developing approach often set by representatives of the Peace-Building agenda. Thus, the rule of thumb would rather be that *in a multi-polar society rules for dialogue between groups are a fundamental trust-building feature.* The Peace-Building agenda is appropriate for developing this. When such a system exists, there is a platform for introducing issues that, for instance, can relate to the defense of human rights.

This would then be an example of twinning, where peace-building begins with a common ground for dialogue. After that, issues of human rights can be brought to the fore and demands can be based on the joint platform's unifying capacity.

SUMMARY

As we have seen, there are possibilities in the conflict phase to develop a situation where the qualities of the two agendas can be used in a way that they would not be able to achieve individually. Making an *interdependent analysis* is a potential platform for contextual analysis as well as further concrete initiatives. When purposefully *giving hope* by showing that action is "always" possible by one agenda or the other, the confidence in the work of the civil society is improved. This is close to what *preparing change* also means to coordinate different types of actions, from the two agendas' representatives, so that a larger space for action is created.

Some of these things may seem "obvious," i.e., uncontroversial and possible to realize without much further ado. There are probably as much obstacles to interdependency, coordination, and joint strategies in the project formulation phase, in headquarters, than there may be in the field.

In the conflict phase—with its urgencies, tensions, and immediate needs—what can and should be done beyond "the obvious"? Is it on any level realistic to think about a strategic dimension of a NGOs work under the conflict phase? There is most likely no easy or generalized response to such questions.

The long-term use in the NGO community of basic analyses that are developed on the level of mutuality in analysis and description—i.e., making an interdependent analysis—will have profound affects on how NGOs can cooperate in the future. The language of the interdependent analysis will set the agenda and language used in subsequent discussions and analyses. This is an intra-NGO consequence. For those affected by the analyzed situations, every step towards a more inclusive analysis should be seen as a development step.

Certain things should be obvious for NGOs and other actors in terms of giving hope. We know that the "horizon of hope" for an individual, a family, a community, or a society is linked to the resources available at any given point in time. To identify at least a preliminary response of why is there a reason to have a hope is obviously a common interest to any NGO working in a conflict phase. Preparing change, for instance, may very well have a "tactical possibility." It depends on the timing: parallel initiatives can support each other in a direct way in a local community. One initiative after the other will have different affects, through a longer and probably more gradual impact.

The tension between peace-building and human rights that we have observed—for instance in the UN,[10] in peace processes (such as Colombia), in situations with severe human rights violations (such as in the DRC), or in negotiation processes[11]—is a methodological one, not a principal one. The discussion is not over human rights principles as such, or negotiation practices, but over how to combine the two. Should justice wait till peace is complete, or should peace wait till justice is done? This is one way to formulate the question.

The Third agenda, to summarize, would in relation to this point propose that the international community—including donor organizations, as well as national organizations and local actors—systematically claim that relevant actors make an analysis and argue in terms of *lives-to-be-spared* for the choice of approach in each specific circumstance.

10. See Hannum, "Human Rights in Conflict Resolution".
11. See Anonymous, "Human Rights"; and Gaer, "Reflections on Human Rights."

6

The Third Agenda during a Post-Conflict Phase

WHEN DISCUSSING THE INTERPLAY between human rights and peace-building during the post-conflict phase, we propose to make use of a set of the following—old and new—concepts: *economic and social conditions, back to the truth,* and *establishing transitional mechanisms.* Although we do not stress the order of the concepts in terms of a logical or causal order, we are nevertheless of the opinion that it is not meaningful to develop a concept such as back to the truth if there is not, first, a visible change at hand regarding economic and social conditions. The point is that back to the truth needs to be developed in a situation that is qualitatively different from a conflict situation. It requires a situation that shows signs of fundamental change from what caused the conflict. Only then may people feel compelled and free to express what previously was held back due to insecurity and the polarization of conflict.

MAKING USE OF COMMON ASSUMPTION

"Human rights" establish a minimum dignity for life. "Truth"—individually and/or collectively understood—establishes a basis for interpretation of the past and present, eventually providing meaning and fulfillment. We argue that any attempt to enter the stabilization phase (which follows after this phase) without an explicit and conscious recognition of the importance of truth and human rights as concepts and practices, will be flawed. The concepts go together, but also extend beyond each other. At the same time, one of them cannot do without the other. Therefore, any tension between the agendas is a serious limitation of the potential that can be found in the development of their common potentialities.

MAKING USE OF INTEGRATION

In the post-conflict phase, integration—full, partial, or project-based— will be treated with the help of the concepts of *economic and social conditions, back to the truth*, and *establishing transitional mechanisms*. If no *interdependent analysis* has been done previously it is recommended to do it at this stage.

Improving Economic and Social Conditions

Economic and social conditions are crucial for any change from a conflict society into peaceful relations between groups and individuals. Not least because many conflicts are about economic and social issues; these may also be expressed in terms of justice, identity, or respect. This first stage of the processes within this phase has already been prepared during the previous conflict phase with its inclusion of measures necessary for *preparing change*. Now it is time for change on ground. How can *improving economic and social conditions* be developed? Among the components necessary for an integration approach to these dimensions, the following aspects can be mentioned:

- cost allocations for war turned into civil projects;
- early dividends: vaccination, micro-financing, local development projects;
- investment in relevant police, judiciary, and prison resources;
- realization of relevant health systems, education, and welfare;
- the rights to return, as well as not to return;
- projects for soldiers and families who participate in disarmament, demobilization, and rehabilitation programs—DDR(R);
- rehabilitation of children at war—a challenge for the whole society.

TABLE 7: Goals and Strategies for the Post-Conflict Phase*

	Respect (no interference in the exercise of the right)	Protect (prevent violations from third parties)	Fulfill (provision of resources and the outcomes of policies)
Civil and Political rights	Measures to prevent state actors from committing torture, extra-judicial killings, disappearance, arbitrary detention, unfair trials, electoral intimidation, and disenfranchisement.	Measures to prevent non-state actors from committing violations, such as torture, extra-judicial killings, disappearance, abduction, and electoral intimidation.	*Investment in judiciaries, prisons, police forces, elections, and resource allocations commensurate with ability.*
Economic, Social, and Cultural rights	*Measures to prevent state actors from committing ethnic, racial, gender or linguistic discrimination in health, education and welfare, and resource allocations below ability.*	*Measures to prevent non-state actors from engaging in discriminatory behavior that limits access to health, education, and other welfare provisions.*	*Progressive realization. Investment in health, education and welfare, and resource allocations commensurate with ability.*

* Measures specially discussed in this section are in italics.

The post-conflict phase is a time when ordinary people should be able to feel free from conflict considerations and limitations. As a first condition, they should not have to fear the kind of human rights violations connected with the conflict-phase anymore. Gradually civil and political rights are available again, or perhaps for the first time. In human rights–based assessments there are two broad categories of human rights included. On the one hand there are the civil and political rights, with guarantees for participation in the political, social, and economic society, including the sanctity for all individuals before the law. On the other hand there are economic, social, and cultural rights including the right to food, health, habitat, economic security, education, the right to a family, cultural affiliation, and collective identity.

In the world today there is a need to be aware of and analyze certain rhetoric on human rights in post-conflict situations. The respect of human rights is, according to this rhetoric, "the bedrock of genuine security," and when identifying what human rights are about certain rights are in focus. In particular, this rhetoric focuses on what are termed fundamental freedoms. Examples that are given in this context are freedom of expression, freedom of assembly, and freedom of religion.[1] There is a tendency to be rather favorable to government and therefore to risk luring people into the trap that freedom is found only in it. The Human Rights agenda is reduced to addressing civil and political rights, and in the next step civil and political rights are defined as "freedom."

> Using the argument of "freedom" is fraying resulting in lack of freedom for those who have no decision-making power in the (social-)political area. The notion of universal human dignity and the rights to be derived from it were born out of people's real experiences of powerlessness.[2]

In the immediate period of a post-conflict situation, when the violent fighting has been stopped, human rights protection may take another shape in comparison to either the conflict phase or a stabilization phase. Keeping in mind that human rights are still applicable in all their aspects, a post-conflict situation shifts the immediate focus on political and civil rights to economic, social, and cultural rights. Individuals and groups directly in the post-conflict situation are in need of immediate satisfaction of their requirements for basic livelihood, including adequate housing, food, health, etc. The new governmental structure must respect those rights and avoid discriminating against any group as well as protect them from non-state actors who might perform some kind of discrimination.

ALLOCATING FOR CIVIL PROJECTS

Economic and social conditions play a key role in the construction of a peaceful and developing post-conflict society. If there is no visible

1. See for example a USA address to the Human Dimension Implementation Meeting in Warsaw, September 29–October 10, 2008 at http://www.osce.org/documents/odihr/2008/10/34221_en.pdf.
2. Mathwig, *Entitling Human Beings*, 9.

change at hand, in the form of viable political alternatives, new policies, reallocation of resources, and incoming practical and political support, then old structures are likely to remain and the longing for truth is put on hold, since the change is in doubt.

It is a key operational principle to establish concrete interplay between principle and action in the civil society, as well as between policy and practice in the political sphere. This interplay involves parties, duty bearers, rights holders, national minorities, as well as conflict-formed actors—no one should be left aside from an inclusive process. This is necessary for breaking skepticism over a forthcoming post-conflict peace process that many groups have reason to formulate. Individuals and groups, including minorities (national, ethnic, religious), who engage to fight within a conflict, with or without arms, demand to be assured that the peace pays off. A conscious allocation of available civil projects made on a national basis—and not a party basis—is a first measure to ensure stability.

There is an immediate need to identify the most disadvantaged and vulnerable in the new situation, those at risk of being violated, as well as those identified as the duty bearers in the new situation. The new situation needs to come to terms with possible discrimination in health, education, as well as emerging welfare and resource allocations.

EARLY PEACE DIVIDENDS

The peace dividend is the positive economic result from ending conflict. It is not the ending of violence, killing, and starvation that makes the peace dividend, but rather the new activities that are made possible, that creates the dividend. When a conflict ends, there is a need within the post-conflict situation to facilitate economic activity and investment, something that also should involve conflict formed actors. This opens the way for projects and campaigns that are necessary to enable the society to once again flourishing.

This is one of the most critical dimensions in the assessment among broad groups of a population to determine whether peace was "worth it" or not. In particular, in sensitive and criticized processes, both parties have a strong incentive to show that "peace pays."

In spite of this, international organizations—civil society or state-based—often have to be the first to show the new possibilities. Government authorities and the state as a whole often have difficulties showing early and clear results of this kind. Timor-Leste and Guatemala are cases in point in this study.

It is common for governments to explain that expectations among the people and politicians of what the change implies are generally too high, particularly at election time. The international community can, and should, always be alert to this aspect. Micro-financing projects, vaccination campaigns, and literacy and democratization awareness campaigns are all concepts known on a global level that have almost universal applicability. To be prepared for early initiatives is not a difficult thing and it demonstrates that it "pays to make peace."

To go from conflict to post-conflict is a change also for the civil society. Yet neither the same demands, nor the same types of pre-cautions, actions, or perspectives can be applied. If civil society proclaims that there is a big difference between peace and war, this needs to be illustrated somehow in the work and thinking of the civil society. If it can be made clear that ending violence means starting development, the first round of convincing the skeptics is won.

But what can the civil society do? It can do two things: give concrete proposals to local and national governments on how such a concrete linking can be developed, and it can show how to practice it through its own resources.

Is this possible? The civil society is not in charge of governmental development resources. This observation has two sides: international and national NGOs sometimes provide basic services—due to national and international support—to a population to an extent that meets the local needs. Does this, however, serve as a de facto replacement of s government's responsibilities in this area. In other situations, the civil society is totally dependent on locally raised resources, thus making it very limited in resource-demanding initiatives. However, if we limit ourselves to NGOs that work with support coming from international cooperation, some linking should be possible to develop.

As examples of such peace dividend projects, based on the types of measures indicated in the list above, one can mention linking together such issues as:

- post-conflict security *with* dialogues over the right to return;

- ending of violence *with* repaired local market and transportation systems;

- disarmament and demobilization *with* individual and family support;

- regional stability *with* micro-finance projects;

- return of refugees *with* compensation for both refugees and non-refugees;

- reduction of security costs *with* increased social/economic development.

INVESTING IN THE SECURITY SECTOR

Is the security sector—i.e., police, judiciary, prison system, national intelligence—an economically relevant sector in society? It represents better than most other parts of a society the difference in kind and therefore in responsibility between the state and the civil society. This fact makes the security sector no less relevant for the civil society, including its business sector, to address, monitor, and at times support when interests are overlapping. A well-trained police, soldiers knowledgeable about human rights and IHL, and respect for human rights in the prison system are fundamental elements with clear implications for combating corruption, fraud, and money laundering, just to mention three examples. As for social life in other sectors, a viable economy and a viable social fabric requires a security sector working with, and not against, the civil society in all its parts.

HEALTH, EDUCATION, AND WELFARE

It is probably not a bad guess that this sector, on a global level, has the strongest representation of civil society organizations and activities. Its importance for human and social development is a "historical fact" while at the same time it is notoriously difficult to measure, quantify, or compartmentalize in a controlled way. Therefore, it is often exposed to ideological pressure and experiments.

The civil society can, by claiming international human rights standards, set a baseline for social conditions in an emerging peaceful society. This creates a clear and non-partisan approach to fundamental issues of dignity.

THE RIGHT TO RETURN AND NOT RETURN

The right to return, or to abstain from returning, is for many a combination of economic and social conditions. Peace-building attempts to bring a divided community back to cooperation and trust may require much longer time than the waiting for a new house, a nearby resettlement, or a final move to another region or another country can allow. To see the interrelationship between economy and social relations is critical with respect to matters of displacement, return, and resettlement. The claim for justice in the post-conflict situation has specifically to deal with the rights of the *refugees and internally displaced people.*

DDR(R) FOR SOLDIERS, FAMILIES, AND CHILDREN

DDR(R) processes—*disarmament, demobilization, rehabilitation,* and *reconstruction*—are, or rather should be, seen as mechanisms for the transfer of power and control into civilian hands. In practice this is in most cases not so. If one side of those involved in the process does not need to demobilize, for instance because they represents a legitimate government, this process is regarded as an asymmetric and power-loosening process as long as the security dilemma is not dealt with. Therefore a different and mutual approach, incorporating a contribution from the Third agenda, is to combine power transfer with DDR(R). This has only happened in one of the cases studied in this project—Timor-Leste—whereas in all other cases DDR(R) has been failing or unsuccessfully coordinated with the political side of the process.

A special dimension of DDR(R) is the *child soldier*, i.e., children and adolescents who are—often involuntarily—involved in fighting and killing. To deal with the experiences of these groups is a particular, difficult, and culturally specific challenge.

Back to the Truth

How can a process of back to the truth be constructed? Which components make up a basis for answering this question? For instance they can be:

- to identify and prosecute serious perpetrators—nationally or internationally (criminal courts, special courts, special panels, etc.);
- to give space and time to mourn and remember (memorial buildings, sacred places of souls, museums, places for naming victims, etc.);

- to compensate victims;

- to establish a *common truth* (via different parties, processes, aspects, rights holders and duty bearers, and/or victims and perpetrators);

- to deal with the question of amnesty and impunity.

IDENTIFYING AND PROSECUTING SERIOUS PERPETRATORS

Accountability of human rights violations in a past conflict is a major theme, both internally and internationally. States, as duty bearers, have a responsibility to prosecute violations against their own laws and against human rights conventions. If and when states are not interested in, or capable of, doing so, the international community has a responsibility to claim justice. In order to do so a number of special courts/panels have been established in the recent decades to prosecute the most serious violations committed in specific conflicts, such as in the former Yugoslavia, Rwanda, Sierra Leone, and Timor-Leste. While these courts are temporary, the establishment of the International Criminal Court in 2002 makes it the first permanent court of its kind. It has the mandate to end impunity for the most serious crimes, in particular genocide, crimes against humanity, and war crimes.

In addition to these crimes, there are a number of violations of human rights as well as crimes according to national laws that need to be accounted for. The human rights–based approach demands compliance with human rights standards and International Humanitarian Law, with the implication of delivering punishment through national, regional, or international courts. This demand is unconditional in crimes such as genocide, crimes against humanity, war crimes, and gross violations of human rights by either one party or both (all) in a conflict where human rights have been violated. There is a clear message that no impunity is acceptable, even if the parties involved agree to provide it. The perpetrators need to be identified and placed in custody in order to face a national trial or international tribunal. There is an obvious need to address and establish an accountability of past crimes.

Finally, in a situation of claiming accountability many groups need special attention. As we have identified above, this can often be women and children. Another such group is child soldiers, whose fate is often both tragic and serious. This makes them not only perpetrators but also victims and rights holders in many respects.

Mourning and Remembering

The balance between looking into the past and/or looking into the future is not so much a question of cooperation between human rights and peace as it is between a retributive and reconciliatory approach to the past. Although this is not a study of reconciliation or political forgiveness, nor is about claiming justice or tribunal justice, there remains a problem of balancing between digging deeper and deeper—through legal processes, reparation claims, and truth commissions—into the "soul" of a nation and the need for looking forward to a future where past atrocities are no longer even a potential reality. No one would argue for a one-sided approach to this, but at the same time, finding an appropriate balance between these two perspectives is a constant challenge.

Establishing a Common Truth

Transitional justice is a concept containing both legal and non-legal mechanisms aimed at achieving truth, justice, and human rights in a post-conflict situation. The field has developed in the wake of the truth and reconciliation commissions established in Africa and Latin America in the 1980s and 1990s, of which the commissions in Chile, Argentina, and South Africa stand out as the most well known. Also, significant work has been carried out by commissions in Timor-Leste, Liberia, Sierra Leone, and other places in recent years.

Most of these commissions have not had a legal mandate; the South African commission is an exception in this aspect and it is not a typical case. Normally, such commissions work with the aspects of truth, reconciliation, and reparation for victims.

"Reconciliation" was introduced as a concept in the political sphere through commissions and processes in the 1980s and 1990s, in both Latin America and Africa. The idea of reconciliation on a national level—between groups, individuals, and states—was based on the assumption that if there is truth there is a possibility for a wider understanding and, in the end, a reassessment of former relations: "my history cannot be understood without yours, and vice versa."

In particular in South Africa, the concept of forgiveness was given a central role—"no future without forgiveness" was the theme elaborated in

particular by Bishop Desmond Tutu.[3] This development—linking reconciliation with forgiveness—has challenged some human rights defenders
who, for instance, would claim that if it means that legal responsibility is
given up, one is mixing the personal level of (possible) forgiveness with
a society's claims for justice on a collective level.

The concept of truth plays a critical role in all reconciliation
processes—this is a common denominator for them all. In practice this
means that seeking truth, for instance through storytelling, taking statements, and public hearings, has a central place in the work of such commissions. Many of them have published reports of thousands of pages
describing in detail events and processes during a period in a nation's
history.

Reconciliation through truth seeking, truth presentation, and
"truth digestion" is a new political phenomenon developing in the last
recent three decades. It is not comparable to the habit of governments
to sometimes publish "white papers" over certain sensitive or critical
events. Instead, they give a wide account based not only on official but
also individual experiences and local events.

The value of such processes is of course not limited to the possibility of individual or group reconciliation, but it also gives a context and
sometimes specific information for legal processes. This relationship—
between the legal and social needs in reconciliation—is a matter of
concern to some, and there are examples of outright tension between
reconciliation commissions and international courts over this particular aspect.[4]

Today, no major peace agreement is without some reference to a
reconciliation mechanism. It has become a standard component in
peace-building. This does not, however, preclude grey zones of mandate
and competence in relation to other processes: legal or political. This
is relevant in particular cases where there are attempts at establishing
reconciliation with a truth component while there is still conflict on national level, such as in the case of Colombia or Palestine.

It is not an exaggeration to say that this is cross-culturally experienced. For any social action, at some level a degree of truth is required
as a precondition. It is recognized that without truth neither justice nor

---

3. Tutu, *No Future*.

4. In Sierra Leone there was a controversy between the two mechanisms, the Special
Court and the Reconciliation Commission, on the status and use of witnesses.

reconciliation is possible. Therefore, the capacity for truth in a society sets a limit for both reconciliation and justice. Both the Human Rights and Peace-Building agendas have, from this point of departure, a starting point of joint work for "truth"—in all its different meanings, from the logical, verifiable, and individually based truth to the collective, inconsistent, and partial but deeply felt common understanding of truth. The different concepts of truth do not in themselves invalidate the yearning and the wish to establish truth.

Some post-conflict societies have a functioning and gradually improving capacity for truth, including a judiciary process, while others remain deeply entrenched in serious problems of politicized legal processes, corruption, and individual protection. The capacity for truth is, in such societies, weak and can sometimes be more effectively developed within the civil society and in non-formal settings than through the formal system. If truth is a fundamental requirement, then the civil society needs to support both the formal and informal sectors pursuing its establishment. In itself the civil society is—this is our assumption—a capacity for truth. What "civil" is in the concept of civil society is among other things the belief in human rights, non-violent methods of work, and respect for the individual's capacity to take initiatives, have an opinion, and act on this premise within the framework of democratic laws and justice.

Therefore, the power-based system for truth-making through the legal system (police, courts, prisons) is always under a double scrutiny from the civil society: when competent, able, and impartial it can be supported; when corrupt, partial, and ineffective it needs to be criticized. The same is true for the informal truth seeking systems that may exist in a society: traditional methods, local practices of sharing, or forcing individuals to reveal information. If voluntary, trusted, and safe for those involved, these methods can be the de facto and only effective sources of truth in a society.

Compensate Victims

The compensation for victims' suffering takes place in at least four different forms. They can be *individual* and/or *collective*, and they can be *symbolic* or *remunerative*. The number of persons who can claim compensation obviously influences its form. Also, when available knowledge is weak or contradictory, or when the moral complexity is high, for instance due to a protracted conflict situation, these are aspects that also influence the nature of compensation. Among truth and reconciliation commissions (see below) there is generally a tendency to set aside the compensatory aspect of work, in favor of other needs. This can be seen if one takes a broad view of a large number of recent commissions, including the well-known case of South Africa.

QUESTIONS OF AMNESTY AND IMPUNITY

Accountability of the past is an important human rights–based issue for rights holders persecuted, oppressed, and discriminated against. How are legal processes established as well as restoration and reparation enabled? The other side of the coin is what to do with former perpetrators of serious human rights violations.

Connected to this problem is *a culture of impunity* developed during some conflicts. Sometimes the question is widened, as in the DRC, when questioning "justice" for perpetrators and victims only occurs when a whole population is unjustly treated. It is the question of impunity, through powerless courts, political agreements, or just failure to act that is the critical issue: the procedures and forms may shift between national and international levels.

One aspect of the possibility to act against impunity is the degree of support from the national and international community to actually undertake action. The position of those accused of war crimes can in a local society be one of a hero, a defender, or someone who would betray a community if he or she accepts responsibility. This is a dimension that is a challenge to both agendas; it is an advocacy question with repercussions for state agencies such as the police and court system.

Amnesty is another concept that sooner or later becomes part of the discussion in the context of this study. Here we are not concerned with cases of "self-amnesty," for instance through decisions by outgoing military governments (El Salvador, Chile, Argentina), but amnesty as a reward for laying down weapons. From a peace-building perspective amnesty is ineffective and not "liked" by negotiators, not only because of the morally dubious aspect of amnesty—justice is made neither for the victim nor the perpetrators—but also for the difficulty of implementing it. Even members of the former military governments of Chile and Argentina, for instance, are not safe from new or renewed cases against them, as we have seen in recent years. Any amnesty, for this reason, is only temporary. A second strong argument is the fact that, from a legal point of view, in certain war crime rules, such as crimes against humanity, and for many other crimes, amnesty would be a severe denigration of justice for victims and the society. This view on amnesty should not be mixed up with the possibility of adjusting final sentences in criminal cases for reasons of cooperation, providing information and general "good behavior." That kind of reduction of sentences is well established and not contested as such.[5]

Establishing Transitional Mechanisms

When treating *establishing transitional mechanisms* as a separate concept we do it against a background of developing economic and social conditions and a *back to the truth* process emerging. The purpose of transitional mechanisms is to bridge to the stabilization phase. How can *establishing transitional mechanisms* bridge the gap between post-conflict and stabilization phases? A few examples are:

- monitoring parties' new respect for human rights;
- mechanisms and resources for democratic elections;
- building up the national capacity (police forces, monitoring, hospitals, commissions);
- transition of international involvement;
- special courts finish and hand over to ordinary judicial systems;
- finalizing institutions for memorialization.

MONITORING PARTIES' NEW RESPECT FOR HUMAN RIGHTS

The post-conflict phase is based on a peace commitment, which means showing new respect for human rights. On this basis, human rights organizations take upon themselves the duty of monitoring the parties of the former conflict to ensure they do not continue with the "old behavior," whenever it meant a violation of human rights. This includes the naming of power structures and mechanisms of control (duty bearers) that ignore an active human rights implementation. In the protection of

---

5. With the help of U.S. criminal court TV series, the concept of plea-bargaining is well established, and can be looked upon as an example in the discussion on this point.

human rights they will show the importance of removing current obstacles for enabling the fulfillment of human rights obligations.

Mechanisms and Resources for Democratic Elections

Mechanisms for establishing democratic elections can be primary movers in the process from conflict to peace-building, since they deal with an event (elections) that is a necessary basis for creating legitimacy for a new order. At the same time they should be institutionalized, and ready to operate regularly, for one election after the other.

Building Up the National Capacity

The lack of developed governmental institutions, including the judicial apparatus as well as other adequate institutions, will in an initial post-conflict phase affect the implementation of human rights. Still, human rights violations on local, regional, and national levels need to be addressed. But equally important is a plan for and realization of the re-building or building up of an apparatus enabling the respect, implementation, protection, and fulfillment of human rights.

The transitional mechanisms are bridging an institutional gap between the post-conflict and stabilization phases. In order for these mechanisms to function they must go hand in hand: a police force that is illiterate is not an effective one, while a justice system without educated functionaries is dysfunctional. This is, in principle, not a contested observation. It is also in line with the view that human rights principles are interrelated—one reinforces the other, violating one negatively affects another. It is for this reason and for general principles of justice that a normative position for the Third agenda is that transitional mechanisms should be fundamentally coordinated in terms of resources, activities, and principles, to the benefit for the country as a whole. This view can also be argued from the point that when the transitional mechanisms finish their work in their capacity as transitional, they should hand over to a normalizing state and society a well-coordinated administrative infrastructure.

The civil society needs individuals (staff, lay functionaries, and committed citizens) that have both a practical and theoretical capacity. Any civil society organization will have to work both internally as well as externally with these issues. Democratization of one's own way of working is both an example and a testing ground for advocacy and educational initiatives in the society at large.

Generally, the transitional mechanisms face the risk of being partial rather than wide-ranging on particular issues, in particular regions, and on particular groups. The greater the lack of resources is, the greater the risk for a patchwork implementation of policies.

Transition of International Involvement

The post-conflict phase is often "ridden by internationals," meaning that in virtually every sector of society there is an international component present—whether through state or non-state cooperation. This is so not only in the fields of human rights and peace-building, but in almost every sector of society. Of course, this is and should be a temporary presence. It is needed before a stabilization based on internal capacities can take place, in order to initiate a clear handing over of responsibilities and resources at the national level. While an election may take place under international guidance and supervision, as part of a transitory arrangement, this event—so fundamental for national independence—has to be organized nationally.

Special Courts Handover to Ordinary Judicial Systems

In the judiciary systems there is also a set of transitional mechanisms, the most well known of which are the special panels or the ad hoc courts for a special conflict, such as in former Yugoslavia and Rwanda.

It is important to notice here that there has been a combination of an institutionalization of the implementation of human rights and IHL on the one hand, and the development of transitional justice instruments on the other.

Finalizing Institutions for Memorialization

The concept of "transitional" has frequently been used to illustrate the special conditions that exist in post-conflict situations. Peace agreements are seen as transitional documents,[6] the economy is in a transitional stage, a constituent assembly is a transitional legislative body, and the justice system has developed a particular field of transitional justice.[7]

6. Bell, *Peace Agreements*.
7. Teitel, *Transitional Justice*.

Basically this development shows sensitivity to the very special conditions that exist right after the end of armed conflict and political turmoil. It is, however, easier to identify the beginning of a transitional phase than its end.

Finalizing institutions for memorialization identifies important turning points in the change from conflict to peaceful development. This is illustrated by handing over from international to national agencies in order to close chapters in one's own history and pave the way for a development that is not marked by that history. Here we need to reflect on the difference between an individual person's ability and will to organize and come to terms with his/her own history on the one hand, and on the other hand the capacity of the society as a whole to both recognize its past and close those moments of history that are barriers to future development. This is always a sensitive balancing act. It can be said that a society must never forget, while an individual can, for her or his personal life, allow things of the past to be put aside. As long as there is sense of truth and justice established, this is likely to be much more possible than it would be otherwise.

MAKING USE OF TWINNING

With the establishment of the category *back to the truth*, we utilize the twinning possibility that exists with the approaches of "accountability for the past" and "reconciliation" from the two original agendas. These are among the major issues of concern for possible tension or conflict between the two original agendas. This can be exemplified by the aim of the Human Rights agenda for punishing perpetrators, and the aim for reconciliation in the Peace-Building agenda.

The *back to the truth* concept is an attempt at handling this tension. It takes its point of departure in the identification of what can be called a society's capacity for truth. A society—with or without open social conflict—has both a formal and informal capacity to bring to light or otherwise establish facts, interpretations, and theories that taken together are regarded by some as "truth." This is not the place for a philosophical discussion about the concept of truth. Here the point is that some pieces of information may simply carry such political, moral, or social weight that the fundamental coherence of a society is threatened if *at a certain point in time* they are presented in an open and factual manner. The formal capacity to bring out truth is represented by independent research capacities, police and judiciary functions, and different types of media. The informal capacity is represented by the ability to analyze and understand—critically or less critically—what rumors, friends, and different types of actions may convey. This is an example on a schematic level of how it can be possible to think and act. Let's do it as steps in a process through which we can construct two processes in order to exemplify this point.

Example 1: Truth and Justice

No peace agreement is developed between combating parties, but the conflict subsides. The Human Rights agenda introduces a truth commission, with the only purpose to be establishing facts and figures. On the basis of this commission's work, the cruelty of the conflict is exposed and the mentality of the society moves towards justice—maybe compensation for victims and legal processes against perpetrators. The Peace-Building agenda supports this initiative but is not a prime mover.

When this new level of consciousness has been established in a society, the Peace-Building agenda introduces a dialogue and conciliation process based on a truth commission—a nationwide social dialogue about the conflict history opens, and individual war leaders appear in public and break their wall of silence. A new level of understanding is reached and a national consensus is developed on how to deal with the final leaders and their violations. The Human Rights agenda supports this, but is not a primary mover.

Example 2: Compensation

On the basis of a Peace-Building agenda a peace commitment is developed so as to include a strong dimension of compensation for victims, not least economically. From a Human Rights agenda, demands for equal justice for everybody are expressed and articulated as a demand, but not as a demand to be included in the agreement.

After the agreement is closed, claims for economic justice are made from a Human Rights agenda and these are based on the peace agreement's provisions. The materialization of victims' compensations generally strengthens the process. At this point, both the Human Rights and the Peace-Building agendas utilize the prospects for also bringing the worst perpetrators to justice.

Hopefully it is possible to think in this synergistic fashion among representatives of the two agendas. Thus, someone affiliated with one agenda or another should be able to imagine and develop a twinning approach.

SUMMARY

During the post-conflict period, *common assumption, integration,* and *twinning* serve as critical approaches for a functioning and cooperating society. As indicated above, the order between the concepts—*improving economic and social conditions, back to the truth,* and *establishing transitional mechanisms*—is not without importance. This idea is based on the assumption that conflict in most cases is about economic and/or social issues. In this phase, we seek a way to diminish the impact of the conflict and, therefore, it is important to specifically address these matters. If not, the truth-seeking or reconstruction of the society as a whole can hide the cause of the original conflict, with its corollaries. This, of course, is important to avoid.

Trying to establish an account of what has happened and why that is as widely accepted as possible is a method that has been applied in tense situations for the purpose of reducing tensions and laying a basis for other initiatives. It is often a component in truth and reconciliation commissions to make a factual/empirical and historical/political analysis of a violent period, its events and background. Also, in attempts to reduce mirror images and stereotypes, historical projects have dealt with mutual texts on the histories and relationships between East and West in Central Europe, as well as between China and Japan. These are, in a way, examples of a tactical application of the idea of *back to the truth*. It is limited in its scope, in expectation of what will be the result, but it functions as a springboard for reassessments, debates, and future actions, also in the field of human rights.

A very important issue moving between a tactical and a strategic consideration is raised when there needs to be a decision on what to do with perpetrators and victims in a post-conflict situation. If we maintain the principle of the right to life, and the principle that truth and human rights always need to go together, we also realize that there are situations when the truth is possible to reveal under informal conditions (e.g., storytelling). In other situations the truth is presented in a formal setting (e.g., courts). Sometimes one cannot wait for truth, but needs to wait for the formal arrangements to be established. In other situations, the formal arrangements are strong enough to bring out truth. At the same time, there may still be a need to go further, beyond the formal aspects, and allow for individual and group perspectives on truth to be encouraged. As a whole, these things would then complement each other and not be allowed work against their deepest interests. It may be a question of tactics, while keeping the long-term strategic goal in mind.

It is easy to focus only on victims and perpetrators. As we have indicated above, there are groups in a society that can neither be identified as parties, victims, or perpetrators, but who change their lives in order to survive, and sometimes even benefit from, an ongoing conflict—*the conflict-formed actors*. These groups also need to assess their life experience. Many of them ask the questions: Did I do the right thing? Did I follow my deepest convictions? Why did I not join one side or the other? Among the conflict-formed actors there are also issues both of responsibility and of an existential nature that need to be addressed.

Finally, while the conflict-formed actor's role changes with the different conflict phases, it is true for the Third agenda concepts of common assumption, integration, and twinning that they are probably most visible in the post-conflict phase. This phase is the one that raises the largest number of challenges to the agenda, and therefore requires the clearest responses. Thus, transitional mechanisms need to be strong enough to give confidence, but "weak" enough to be either dismantled or turned into permanent structures. This is the issue that arises in the next and final phase, the stabilization phase.

7

The Third Agenda During a Stabilization Phase

WITH THE STABILIZATION PHASE the society enters into being a more "normal" society, hopefully based on the rule of law and a democratic system. In the beginning of this phase the Third agenda is still important as a tool, but gradually fades into the background as more stabilization is achieved and human rights and peace-building, respectively, can establish a position in their own capacities. Still, the stabilization phase also faces the risk that things can go wrong. The old conflict may return if basic issues were not settled, new conflicts can still easily be created, and, most probably, new issues will come onto the political agenda that are likely to put pressure on key institutions and actors in the society. This will still give the Third agenda a role, taking into account the need for education, capacity-building, and theoretical and methodological considerations, not least for the reason that the conflict should never "be allowed" to return.

MAKING USE OF COMMON ASSUMPTION

Every society "at peace with itself" is practicing a level of mutual acceptance and *trust* in the behavior towards other individuals and groups. If not, this society would not function and certainly not develop more advanced systems of belief, cooperation, and long-term planning.

Conflicts and armed conflicts, in particular, deprive individuals and groups of the means for cooperation and make a point in creating mistrust. Mistrust is part of the conflict process. Trust, then, is the key mechanism and principle by which a stabilizing society must be built. The challenge is not to formulate this principle, but to put it into practice. How can trust be experienced?

A principle of trust for building a society can be formulated as a number of "rules of thumb" for stabilization:

- trust as the first attitude, until the opposite is deemed necessary;

- trust as the first proposal, until the opposite is deemed necessary;

- trust as the first goal of joint action, until the opposite is deemed necessary;

- trust as what should be deepened in a relation, until the opposite is deemed necessary.

Rules of thumb like these can be used as points of reference for establishing a norm for inter-group relations in a conflict-prone society. Probably they work as points for discussing more than anything else: Who, if anyone at all, can be trusted in our society?

If they serve this purpose, the rules of thumb are sufficient. The point is that when human rights and peace are to be established, a new culture based on these concepts also needs to be established. Trust is a key concept in this agenda of the stabilization phase.

MAKING USE OF INTEGRATION

Based on the Human Rights and Peace-Building agendas, making use of *integration* in the Third agenda during the stabilization phase can be based on these concepts: *establishing norms*, *building institutions*, and *experiencing trust*. These three concepts are used here for getting integration between the agendas.

The stabilization phase is always exposed—at least theoretical—to the risk of a backlash. Conflicts can be revived, actors can return in new guises, and the implementation of a peace process can be weak or faulty. Thus there is a need for supporting a solid combination of fundamental human rights and peace-building principles. For this reason, even if the situation allows for greater freedom to be developed, is critical for the two agendas to maintain cooperative stances and utilize available common ground.

Establishing Norms

Establishing norms is here used as a concept for indicating a need for permeating the society with the norms of the Human Rights agenda, as well as in the Peace-Building agenda. This is done through developing a culture of human culture and a culture of democracy existing in an integrated situation. Hopefully, this is achieved through pinpointing education and capacity-building of the entire society as key processes. How can establishing norms be realized? Obviously, on the normative level there is significant unanimity between the two cultures—the human rights culture and the culture of democracy—even if differences and different priorities can be identified. Establishing norms can include the following aspects:

- capacity-building of national and long-term staff in human rights and democracy;
- civil society giving service and lobbying beyond immediate stakeholders;
- taking local responsibility for priorities and norms;
- human rights empowerment through education for everyone (reciprocal understanding between rights holders and duty bearers);
- taking into account gender dimensions and power structures in the normative system;
- empowerment in processes of democracy and elections through education;
- non-discrimination against marginalized and minority groups (national, ethnic, religious, etc.);
- mechanisms for managing frictions and local conflicts.

In a situation of increasing capacity-building a core obligation is to satisfy a minimum essential level for each human right. One human right that can be given priority in this phase is education. It can function as a catalyst for the fulfillment of many human rights, as well as giving clear definition of the relationship between rights holders and duty bearers for establishing a healthy relationship between them.

TABLE 8: Goals and Strategies for Human Rights in the Stabilization Phase*

	Respect (no interference in the exercise of the right)	Protect (prevent violations from third parties)	Fulfill (provision of resources and the outcomes of policies)
Civil and Political rights	Measures to prevent state actors from committing torture, extra-judicial killings, disappearance, arbitrary detention, unfair trials, electoral intimidation, and disenfranchisement.	Measures to prevent non-state actors from committing violations, such as torture, extra-judicial killings, disappearance, abduction, and electoral intimidation.	*Investment in judiciaries, prisons, police forces, elections, and resource allocations commensurate with ability.*
Economic, Social, and Cultural rights	Measures to prevent state actors from committing ethnic, racial, gender or linguistic discrimination in health, education and welfare, and resource allocations below ability.	Measures to prevent non-state actors from engaging in discriminatory behavior that limits access to health, education, and other welfare provisions.	*Progressive realization. Investment in health, education and welfare, and resource allocations commensurate with ability.*

* Measures specially discussed in this section in italics.

Here we can list key questions for an analysis of what is necessary for implementing a human rights issue.[1]

1. Human rights concern

   - What specific human rights of claim holders are being affected? What are the specific elements of such rights?

   - Would women have different concerns aside from or other than the concerns of men?

   - Did women and men experience the situation differently?

---

1. This follows closely *Rights-Based Approach*, 81–84.

- What specific human rights principles are weak and affecting the rights of claim holders?

2. Weaknesses and vulnerabilities

   a. Rights holders

   - Which groups have least access to resources/power? Do they face discrimination?
   - Who are those affected by the adverse consequences of this situation?
   - Who, among those affected, are the most vulnerable? Why?
   - Did women and men experience the situation differently?

   b. Duty-bearers

   - Who are the duty bearers for each of the most influential human rights concerns indentified? Who has the capacity to respond to such concerns? Who has the obligation to respond?
   - What are the specific duties of duty bearers with regards to such concerns?
   - What are the duties of claim holders?

   c. Underlying causes

   - What are the structures/events/actions/attitudes/behaviors that can cause/reinforce such weaknesses and vulnerabilities?

   d. Levels of action

   - What are the levels of action and the desired results (individual, community, policy, institutional—local/national)?

This phase is an implementation period for rebuilding or building up a national human rights infrastructure giving all human rights a possibility to coexist. What was inaugurated during the post-conflict phase will now continue with building functioning governmental institutions including a judicial apparatus and other adequate institutions enabling civil and political rights. This is basically the introduction of democracy and good governance.

In this phase unjust structures in the society are addressed. Structures oppressing rights holders may be changed to give people possibilities to form their society. This is very much about social and economic rights as initiated in the post-conflict phase. A part of the cause to the violent conflict may, together with other factors, involve social and economic issues when a population is sharply divided and individuals or groups believe they are worse off than their relevant reference groups.[2] In any situation when a significant portion of a population are deprived of economic and social rights like food, water, housing and health it is the duty of the state to call upon all available resources including international assistance. In the beginning of the capacity-building phase the urgent needs for survival and freedom from starvation must be satisfied, followed by a progressive building of greater infrastructure over time. This process needs to be transparent and participatory, aiming to reflect a consensus between rights holders—those whose rights are being violated—and duty bearers—those with a duty to act. But it is as much a process of involving the marginalized and people without power in the decision-making processes and enabling power sharing when changing of oppressing structures.

Taking into Account Gender Dimensions and Power Structures

"Stabilization," as a concept, has an aura of conservatism and traditionalism. When things stabilize they go back to what they used to be. In relation to gender aspects of life and society, and in relation to matters that require close monitoring concerning the gender dimension, it becomes important to ask: What will make the new situation different from the past?

There are some unfortunate developments that have an impact on gender relations that come directly from a conflict itself. Many men are killed and the men are often at an age of pending or recent family formation. In Rwanda, after the genocide in 1994, the laws for marriage and inheritance were neither updated in relation to gender, nor dealing fully with the parallel mono- and polygamous marriage practices of the country.

"Inheritance" is a social practice that in effect borders the power structure dimension. Women may be strong landholders if inheriting

2. Thoms and Ron, "Do Human Rights Violations," 674–705.

their husbands killed in the war. The close relation between gender and power is here conspicuous. The stabilization phase need monitoring when it comes to the content of laws and regulations, and a grassroots process in order to anchor values and practices that are both generally accepted and promoting the rights of women and children, in particular.

EMPOWERMENT FOR DEMOCRACY AND ELECTION

A critical factor in the post-conflict phase is, as we have seen, the need for visible and somewhat steady improvement of life conditions. The stabilization phase is challenged with the task to pick up and make stable, or even institutionalize, what is still remaining from the first peace-building and human rights–inspired projects in the post-conflict phase. If the first projects were built on international or existing national capacity, this is the time for capacity-building of national and long-term staff. Stability is now established to a degree where initiatives that were begun in the previous phase are now being institutionalized, such as micro-loan institutions, industrial training, improved agricultural methods, accounting and auditing standards, road projects, telephone and communications systems, etc.

The kind of developments we see within the civil society here refer to its own institutionalization (such as associations of civil society organizations), taking on secondary tasks to give service beyond their immediate stakeholders (such as facilitate in social tension situations), lobbying for particular legislation, and taking on international commitments.

The Human Rights agenda has a number of principles that could serve almost as a "textbook" with the first chapter being peace-building capacity training. However, the second chapter would deal with managing friction, frustration, local conflicts, and serious threats. How can conflicts over resources be practically resolved when there are no resources immediately available? This and similar issues are typical peace-building concerns in a phase where stabilization is based on a day-to-day presence of all constructive forces.

NON-DISCRIMINATION

Of course, it could be argued that national minorities are protected satisfactorily through the implementation of the human rights systems when they are realized during the post-conflict and stabilization phases. But the history of conflicts and wars speaks in a language of special vulnerability when it comes to minorities inside a state and not least minorities separated between two or more states.

If the issue of a national minority has been a direct part of the conflict, the issue—we assume—has been settled through the post-conflict phase in order to reach the stabilization phase. But it is also possible that a conflict has temporally suppressed minority issues when facing a common enemy and then this minority issue reappears in the stabilization phase.

If so, what is happening to the minority is crucial during the stabilization phase. If the existing violations and discrimination are satisfactorily met there is even a risk of a new conflict and eruption of violence. In order to prevent such a development, recommendations have been issued to deal with the participation of national minorities in the governance of states. The Lund Recommendations from 1999 are applicable in this situation, as are, for instance, the OSCE *Guidelines to Assist National Minority Participation in the Electoral Process*.[3]

MECHANISMS FOR MANAGING FRICTIONS AND LOCAL CONFLICTS

The long-term effects of civil war are recognized but nevertheless are little understood. If inter-community distrust, or even hatred and killings, have been part of a conflict, the trust-building component—with all its dimensions and sensitivities—needs to somehow be addressed. Organizations representing the civil society on both sides of such trust fissures have tasks and responsibilities in such situations. Experiences from such work are widely available today—from Northern Ireland, Palestine, India, Australia, Canada, Latin America, and Africa/South Africa. This is a typical long-term activity, the value of which may not be seen unless serious strain is put upon inter-ethnic relations; something that no one wants to see.

All major wars during the last century were characterized by a significant disproportion between civilian and military casualties. In some wars over 80 percent of the casualties were civilian and in the twenty-first century—even before the period of recent terrorist attacks—there is often a deliberate policy among combatants to target civilians as part of the strategy in armed conflict. The Balkans, Liberia, Sudan, and Sri Lanka are just a few examples of this phenomenon.

---

3. *Guidelines to Assist*, 8.

When civilians are threatened and killed, women and children, together with the elderly, normally make up the largest portion of these victims. Women are particularly exposed in civil wars, where the soldiers—from either side—may use the civilian population (primarily women) for providing food, shelter, and sexual purposes. Many civil wars are examples of a grim combination of sexual abuse and physical violations at the same time.

Conflicts are about power. There is a reality of power, in the political as well as human spheres, that penetrates all levels in conflict settings. Gender relations have a power dimension as well, and it is an often-observed fact that former soldiers bring their attitudes and behavior from the war back into their private lives and the domestic relations in their own households. This is not necessarily related to psychological problems (such as post-traumatic stress disorders) but it is an expression of a new set of attitudes.

These observations point towards the need for a thorough and systematically applied gender-based analysis as part of other analytical and practical approaches in post-conflict situations. This may be made in an integrated way as well as a separate approach, depending on the specific need.

Building Institutions—From Village to Parliament

Building institutions is yet another practice of the concept of *integration*. In a new culture characterized by an integrated human rights culture and a culture of democracy, the norms need to find an expression through concrete institutions aiming at protecting, developing, and, not least, implementing the new culture.

Which components are crucial in building institutions? Sometimes the norms precede institution-building and sometimes the institutions are in place to promote the norms. Using integration the following points may be taken into account:

- building a national human rights infrastructure;
- building a national structure for peace and security;
- investment in judiciaries, police forces, etc.;
- realization of basic education, health, and welfare systems;
- identifying institutions dealing with rights holders' situations

(groups with least access to power, facing discrimination, living in vulnerable situations);

- identifying institutional duty bearers in the new situation (in a redefined state who has the obligation and capacity to respond?);

- handing over processes/projects to local partners.

Building National Structures

Normally, the civil society has few or no resources available for involvement in the physical construction of democratic institutions—this is simply not the purpose of a civil society organization. There is, however, a psychological and cognitive dimension to democracy where NGOs have a strong role to play.

How is a parliament working? What does it mean to be elected? Why is corruption called "stealing from the people"? Why is giving up power in an election as democratic a behavior as getting power? Democracy means listening to everybody, also—or in particular!—those you do not agree with. Some have done it before. Sunday Democracy Schools is a parallel idea for churches' Sunday Schools. Maybe they can even be combined?

Investment in Judiciaries, Police Forces, etc.

It is a truism to state that the institutionalization of the fundamental structural mechanisms of a society takes time and resources. Such a statement is easily turned into an overwhelming feeling of lack of capacity and resources for such major undertakings among those that think through these processes. It should, however, not be forgotten that it can be as important for the general public to see that this process has started as it is to see that it has reached all its goals very quickly. Just to take one example: in East Timor, when the United Nations mission administrated the process towards independence from late 1999 to 2002, the establishment of the police academy was a major and symbolically important event. It was very important for the establishment of some level of order. After such a beginning, the gradual achievement of trust and commitment is earned through long-term work.

Realization of Basic Education, Health, and Welfare Systems

Education, health, and certain welfare instruments are identified as human rights. Therefore they cannot be realized only with the eventual will of a government. While the levels of basic education, for instance, cannot be standardized globally in a simplistic way, because it is dependent on differences in available resources, there is no escape for governments that seek to minimize their spending on such issues. Since the development of the human being is severely hampered when health or education are minimized, these are matters of respect for human dignity and are non-negotiable. The single most important dimension to monitor and scrutinize is the principle of *general* access to education, health care, and welfare. After conflict and war those who happen to live in cities or towns more easily have access to these rights than those living in rural areas. Still, a majority of a population often lives in the country side.

Identifying Institutions Dealing with Rights Holders' Situation

The perspective of rights holders is to give the power to the individual without rights and at the same time to all individuals in the same situation—"the people." People are accepted as key actors in their own matters and not just considered to be passive recipients. They have the right to claim responsibility from the duty bearers—the state and, when applicable, non-state actors. Human rights are a reciprocal understanding of complex relationships between rights holders and duty bearers. To build a human rights culture is capacity-building through education and empowerment of duty-bearers to be able to conduct and implement their duties. In the same way, the rights holders should be aware of their right to claim their non-realized rights. Not least this goes for both how one presents their claims and how those claims are met, as well as building appropriate institutions.

Identifying Institutional Duty Bearers in the New Situation

In the stabilization phase the Third agenda faces the risk of being less visible from a methodological point of view. This phase points in two directions with respect to the agendas. From one point of view it is possible for each agenda to be less dependent on the other and to develop its own programs without "bothering" about other perspectives—the feeling would then be that one can have the luxury of being individualistic when things stabilize. Another perspective—which is suggested here—is to say that the issues requiring focus in the stabilization phase become less and less divisive for the two agendas. If, during the conflict phase, there were different views about the role of peace-building and human rights in the midst of violence and violations, the stabilization phase is about institutionalization of human rights in the form of democratic norms and practices. Both agendas support such development, therefore integrating them seems theoretically less of a challenge when compared to the previous phases.

The capacity to use a democratic system is a key aspect of its institutionalization. Here some systems can be based on oral traditions, while others require formal skills. In addition, there always has to be a degree of motivation and interest resulting in mobilization. Peace-building has often been about community mobilization based on common grounds for development and effective resource management within a framework of security, fundamental rights, and democratic values. Taken to the societal level, such a perspective coincides to a high degree with what human rights proponents have long worked for, addressing governmental institutions and the state's representatives themselves. If taken too literally, these two approaches foster a "sectorization" of minds and practices through mere application of their respective programs. To develop a perspective on how a bottom-up approach for social change is working from a village to the parliament requires an integration of the two agendas, something they have the content and experience for doing, but too seldom develop as a conscious practice.

EXPERIENCING TRUST

The Third agenda has played its role for a trusting and fruitful pattern of dealing with human rights and peace-building, both during the conflict phase and the post-conflict phase. In the stabilization phase, however, there may still be need for a long-term development of inter-community trust building. Still, we know that new issues causing conflicts can easily appear and old conflicts reappear. In this situation, every society needs to work on trust-building to avoid possible backlashes. Yet, most important is to develop a strategic approach for facing the present and the future.

How can trust be accentuated between groups in a society under the stabilization phase? Which components are crucial in *experiencing trust*? Using *integration* the following points may be taken into account when considering this:

- protection of minorities;
- electoral systems should not allow parties that are ethnically or religiously uniform;
- school systems and text books should be developed so as to avoid implicit group criticism;
- systematically designed cooperative projects involving groups from different sides need to be formed;
- religious actors should be encouraged to develop interreligious councils for conflict prevention;
- sports activities should be developed so as to bridge potentially divisive lines in national or international sports events.

Cooperative Projects for Inter-Community Trust Building

No one with experience from civil wars regards the cleavages that they create as "forgotten" or "overcome" just because there have been processes of truth, court proceedings, or reconciliation meetings or processes. None of these methods delete from the memory of individuals what has happened—and this may not even be the purpose of these methods. Instead, what they all may contribute to is a way of living with the memories, not against them so to speak.

Therefore, trust-building among and between individuals and groups in the local community, as well as on national level, will continue to be a priority during the stabilization phase as well. Among those cases studied in this report, Timor-Leste is a case where the split and instability between various groups in 2006 showed that reconciliation through various forms a few years before did not achieve the thorough-going change that many donor countries may have hoped for.

Systematic inter-group peace work is, for this reason, an important priority during the stabilization phase. The purpose of such work is then to demonstrate that "combining forces" leads to gains that otherwise would not be possible. Or in other words, again drawing on the example of Timor-Leste, if communities with different political affiliations join their resources they will be eligible for obtaining support which when joined together will enable construction of things beyond their own individual reach, such as a harbor/community house/fishing industry or the like.

The principle of equality becomes a basis for cooperation—cooperation that pays. We should not underestimate the material aspect of this kind of choices among people. Just as economic and material issues play a significant role in elections in industrialized countries, the same perspective is applied by the population in developing countries. Principles gain life from being realized, i.e., by visible linking.

PROTECTION OF MINORITIES

Often minorities or groups based on ethnicity, religion, language, color, HIV status, or economic marginalization experience their right to identity being denied and suppressed in various ways. In many cases, for instance during a conflict phase, a minority or persons belonging to a minority may be exposed to discrimination and/or violations against their human rights. In several conflicts, like in Congo (DRC) and Rwanda, minority characteristics are part of the cause of the conflict. There is also a possibility that minority issues have been temporarily suppressed in the face a common enemy only to reappear in the stabilization phase.

In cases where there are still existing violations and discriminatory situations that are not satisfactorily resolved, there is even a risk of a new conflict erupting followed by new violence. In the stabilization phase it is important to pay attention to tensions between minorities and the majority as well as interethnic tensions. It is necessary that the state deals with the rights of minorities as well as the participation of minorities in the public life and governance of the state.[4]

PROMOTING BROADER UNDERSTANDING

If deep divisions characterize a conflict-ridden society, its peace structure should not follow, or worse entertain, these divisions. School textbooks are conveyors of attitudes and values, and often statements pass without any critical reflection upon their consequences or deeper effect on a society's mentality. There are many examples of projects among historians or teachers that try to formulate a common image of a violent and shared past. This is helpful not only for the students, but for everyone involved.

4. See also the Lund Recommendations from 1999 and the OSCE *Guidelines to Assist National Minority Participation in the Electoral Process.*

Sometimes conflict divisions follow lines of ethnic divisions, and a particularly sensitive case is if this division also overlaps with minorities' rights. An electoral system, for instance established through the formation of electoral districts, or by defining rules for organizing a political party, can create more or less favorable conditions for parties that try to legitimate their policies by utilizing the divisions of the conflict period. Some countries would, for instance, not allow parties to select candidates from only one ethnic group if they want to be elected to the parliament. For this reason, the party has to be at least "bipartisan" in order to get votes. The effect is that this will enforce a certain level of compromises and concern for groups outside one's own.

MAKING USE OF TWINNING

Making use of *twinning* in the stabilization phase may appear as too long-term and a "clumsy" way of organizing development support. This is because the stabilization phase easily seems to have no end, but instead requires that each organization supporting the stabilization develops its own exit plan.

Organizations and groups that in peacetime find space for articulation of their needs and interests often find that when conflict is rampant they are either dismissed or overlooked in other ways. During the stabilization phase it is a duty, from human rights and peace-building perspectives, to bring to the fore groups that have been created or marginalized by the war—such as war veterans, the handicapped, and ethnic, religious, or sexual minorities, HIV/Aids affected, or others stigmatized by war or expulsion. There is still a need for a twinning approach from human rights and peace-building groups in dealing with the situations and rights of minorities. In the stabilization phase it is easy to overlook, due to a general feeling of relief resulting from the improvement of a situation that had been much worse, the fact that there are still groups in a community or society on the whole who still suffer a situation that at their personal level may not be felt to be too different from what the case was during the height of the armed conflict.

As a parallel to the protection of rights, for instance, of marginalized groups, there is a need for twinning for the purpose of establishing democratic norms and practices. For instance, the international community often presents democracy as a system of conflict management that can replace the armed struggle through the ways and means of peaceful political struggle. However, democracy normally means that at least one (group or party) is losing, yet at the same time a loss is always temporary in a democracy. The capacity to lose, to accept loss, and to accept that someone else—even an enemy—is a winner, is a critical democratic skill. No democratic mentality is needed for taking power after even democratic elections. The test comes when power is lost and expected to be handed over to someone else.

By twinning, it is possible to strengthen norms through informal awareness-raising campaigns among voters. There are a number of democratic principles that are required to be addressed specifically in such campaigns, for instance regarding why the biggest party does not always form a government, or that it is the parliament that has the final word and makes the laws, etc. The advantage with twinning comes from the possibility of paving the way among people in general for pushing for specific human rights demands from a government. Informed citizens will have a much higher impact on their government, if and when they have discussed and reflected on the issues beforehand.

Example 1: Organizational Maturity Case

How could one "wait" for the other while change takes years or decades? The answer is that it is the inner activity of the respective organizations that provide the substance for twinning. To give an example: when the police corps has reached a certain level of competence, stability in that society might have reached a certain level too, and at that point there is a possibility to take initiatives. On this basis new ground can be created from one agenda or the other, depending on the issues concerned.

Example 2: Second-Generation Dialogue Case

Likewise, when a second election has been held, dialogues that have been "forgotten" in the pre-election periods can be continued through a Peace-Building agenda, for instance, and thereby establish a ground for recognition and mutuality that enables more truths to see the light of day—given that stability is the common perception of the situation.

SUMMARY

In one way, it is possible to claim that entering into a stabilization phase with some kind of normalization will reduce the importance of a Third agenda. But we claim the importance for the Third agenda also during this phase. The reason is partly due to enabling a society to always be prepared to live with human rights and peace-building. The *common assumption*, *integration*, and *twinning* approaches will make the civil society, as well as the state apparatus, involved in *establishing norms*, *building institutions*, and *experiencing trust* in this phase.

To be strategic under a stabilization phase is to use the stability that exists for the purpose of creating more and long-term stability and peace. From a peace-building perspective this implies institutionalization of democratic institutions based on a wide support of democratic values and principles. From a human rights perspective this means a full recognition and implementation of all relevant human rights conventions and documents for the country under analysis.

It should be recognized the stabilization phase has "no end," but is defined by its transition to permanence and long-term locally managed performance. Its characteristics, then, become visible through the change of minds and practice in a society.

8

Challenges for Constructing a Partnership

THE FRICTION BETWEEN THE Human Rights and Peace-Building agendas—which has been identified by so many practitioners and theoreticians—has here been treated as an operational problem, more than a matter of principles. At a general level, if someone believes that human rights proponents are less interested in peace than are peace-builders, and if the latter should be seen as less interested in human rights implementation than human rights proponents, we think this is a false and incorrect point of departure. Inasmuch as the tensions are an operational problem, this study has at least shown that it is possible to develop significant forms of cooperation, adjusted to the nature of the issue as well as to available resources.

In the initial five critical cases (see chapter 3) as well as in discussing the United Nations (see chapter 1) we basically found the two agendas (the Human Rights agenda and the Peace-Building agenda) living separate lives. This is clearly seen from the way NGOs organize and concentrate their efforts in conflict and post-conflict phases. The work through the Third agenda during the different phases will give new possibilities to act in future conflicts. This is not achieved just by changing the name of an NGO to include both concepts, but through building an organization where the two agendas are integrated into the ongoing work. Internal education and capacity-building will be key issues.

TENSIONS SOLVED THROUGH A THIRD AGENDA?

The tensions that exist can be turned into resources: in themselves they motivate having two agendas, which provide experts in their respective fields and create opportunities for joint action and synergy. The agendas can be said to represent different approaches to specific situations such as: individual versus group orientation; specific roles for duty bearers, rights holders, and parties versus shared responsibility and community trust-building; and principle orientation versus power/persuasion orientation. These all contain qualities that in given situations may very well be complementary and mutually beneficial for overarching goals.

The construction of the Third agenda, with its methodological approaches of *common assumption*, *integration*, and *twinning*, is one example of how the differences of the agendas create a mutually beneficial way of acting. The challenge in constructing a partnership between the agendas lies in the risk of falling back into too narrow a perspective on either side of the specific situation that they are both dealing with.

The main features of the three phases (conflict, post-conflict, and stabilization) in relation to the Third agenda can be summarized as follows:

TABLE 9: Summary of Methodological Approaches in the Third Agenda

	Conflict Phase	Post-conflict Phase	Stabilization Phase
Common assumption	The right to life	Human rights and truth	Trust
Integration	Interdependent analysis; Giving hope; Preparing change	Economic and social conditions; Back to the truth; Establishing transitional mechanisms	Establishing norms; Building institutions; Experiencing trust
Twinning	*Example I*: Justice vs. peace; *Example II*: Polarization case	*Example I*: Truth and justice case; *Example II*: Compensation case	*Example I*: Organizational maturity case; *Example II*: Second generation dialogue case

Basically, what we have done in this study—based on traditional human rights and peace-building approaches—is to find constructive concepts for each and every phase discussed, taking into account parties/victims, rights holders/duty bearers, and conflict-formed actors. Relating to the *conflict* phase we have developed the concepts of *interdependent analysis*, *giving hope*, and *preparing change*. In relation to the *post-conflict* phase (i.e., what occurs after a *peace commitment* is identified) we have elaborated the concepts of *economic and social dimensions*, *back to the truth*, and *transitional mechanisms*, which end up in the phase-defining concept of *rule of law*. The stabilization phase is finally established when rule of law emerges and transitional mechanisms fade away. This phase is discussed through the concepts *establishing norms*, *building institutions*, and *experiencing trust*.

Through the use of three methodological principles of *common assumption* (using overlapping principles such as *the right to life*, *human rights and truth*, and *trust*), *integration* (making a new blend), and *twinning* (preparing the way for each other), we show how an approach for increasing the capacity can be developed when the civil society is working with Human Rights and Peace-Building agendas.

To enable the Third agenda for dealing with processes of "ending conflict and creating peace" —and in doing that to take into account simultaneously human rights–based and peace-building approaches— we suggest:

- a recognition of complementary ideas and working methods;

- a systematic use of the common assumption, integration, and twinning in order to utilize synergy effect possibilities;

- to develop common principles of democracy, human dignity, and social structures through the three overarching principles labeled *right to life*, *human rights and truth*, and *trust*;

- that all education/training that is related to violent conflict must bring together human rights and peace-building approaches;

- that agencies and departments/ministries need to rethink their approaches to securing human rights and peace-building and enable comprehensive solutions when appropriate.

THREE CHALLENGES

The preceding chapters have dealt with some of the challenges that face anyone who wants the two agendas to cooperate and provide synergetic contributions to a society changing from violence and violations to rights and justice.

A *first* challenge is to see how *the complementarity of individual and collective approaches* can be utilized. By definition a society is a collective, while at the same time its most important units are its individual members. There has to be recognition that special attention is needed for dealing with the respective levels. The Human Rights agenda and the Peace-Building agenda have specific contributions to make for the individual and collective levels of a society. Moreover, concepts and practices move from one level to another—a case in point is the concept of "security," which today is not only a matter for states, but has also developed into a wider concept including, for instance, "human security."

A *second* challenge is to see how *a state-oriented approach can be utilized together with a civil society-oriented approach*. Human rights are supposed to be primarily defended by the state—a principle that is not always reflected in actual state behavior. Peace-building, on its part, takes place both at national and local levels through national institution-building and local civil society development. Therefore, peace-building is in some way very similar in its outlook to human rights when implemented on the national level through the support of institution-building such as the establishment of judiciary systems, schools, and hospitals. On the local level, the difference with the Human Rights agenda is more visible due to its orientation towards the civil society as a key actor on that level. This challenge crisscrosses the two agendas of this study. The different roles of the state and of the civil society are reflected respectively in this study in the approach of the Third agenda.

These challenges are theoretical in the sense that they deal with principles of analysis and action in the agendas focused on in this study, but the real challenge lies in implementation. It is then a *third* challenge *to utilize the operational possibilities that are offered by the Third agenda.* When analyzing if there is an advantage to employing two agendas in one single situation openness is a key issue. It allows for a broader set of working options, which, strangely enough, could make the whole project less complicated to realize in the end.

To implement the Third agenda by doing "what should be done" and avoid doing what is "usually done" is not a slogan. When a project is to become a reality and take on specific content, beyond being simply ideological, it requires the hard work of understanding that what is needed in a specific situation cannot be provided by the more or less routine application of a method that "usually works" elsewhere.

Finally, this study is an argument regarding policy. It shows that the tension that sometimes appears between the two agendas can be dealt with in a constructive way. At the same time, there is no explicit road from policy to practice. Yet from conviction can sometimes come new abilities. With respect to the two agendas, it is our view that many constructive forms for cooperation between them are both desirable and possible. We offer one possible way to attain this: the Third agenda.

Bibliography

2011 UNHCR Country Operations Profile—Colombia. UNHCR 2011. Online: http://www.unhcr.org/cgi-bin/texis/vtx/page?page=49e492ad6.

Abiri, Elisabeth. *Let's Talk!—Human Rights Meet Peace and Security*. SIDA report 28896. Stockholm: Swedish International Development Cooperation Agency, 2006. Online: http://www.humanrights.se/articleData/914eb1e478664811ba2171467465 0e6b.pdf.

An Agenda for Peace, Preventive Diplomacy, Peacemaking and Peace-Keeping: Report of the Secretary-General. UN doc. A/47/277; S/24111. June 17, 1992. Online: http://www.un.org/Docs/SG/agpeace.html.

Amnéus, Diana. *Responsibility to Protect by Military Means—Emerging Norms on Humanitarian Intervention?* Stockholm: Department of Law, Stockholm University 2008.

Anderson, Mary B. *Do No Harm. How Aid Can Support Peace—or War*. Boulder, CO: Lynne Rienner, 1999.

An-Na'im, Abdullahi Ahmed. "Towards a More People-Centered Human Rights Movement." In, *Mänskliga rättigheter—från forskningens frontlinjer* (*Human Rights—From the Frontiers of Research*), edited by Diana Amnéus and Göran Gunner. Uppsala: Iustus förlag, 2003.

Annual Report of the Secretary-General on the Work of the Organization (1998). GAOR, 53rd sess., suppl. 1. UN doc. A/53/1. August 27, 1998. Online: http://www.un.org/Docs/SG/Report98/.

Anonymous. "Human Rights in Peace Negotiations." *Human Rights Quarterly* 18.2 (1996) 249–58.

Armyr, Ingmar. *No Shortcuts to Peace. International Development Cooperation, Human Rights, and Peacebuilding*. Research Paper Series 5. Stockholm: Stockholm School of Theology, 2008. Online: http://www.ths.se/research/paper_no5.pdf.

Bell, Christine. *Negotiating Justice?: Human Rights and Peace Agreements*. Geneva: International Council on Human Rights Policy, 2006. Online: http://www.ichrp.org/files/reports/22/128_report_en.pdf.

———. *Peace Agreements and Human Rights*. Oxford: Oxford University Press, 2000.

Castro, Augusto, and Augustinho de Vasconcelos. *Justice and Reconciliation—Two Contexts, Two Reflections*. Research Paper Series 6. Stockholm: Stockholm School of Theology, 2008. Online: www.ths.se/site/images/stories/forskning/paper_no6.pdf.

Chega!: The Report of the Commission for Reception, Truth, and Reconciliation. Dili, Timor-Leste: CAVR, 2005. Online: http://www.etan.org/news/2006/cavr.htm.

Corell, Hans. *Creating a Global Rule of Law Meeting Point*. Online: http://www.havc.se/res/SelectedMaterial/20080129hiil2007annualhiilconference.pdf.

Custers, Raf, and Sara Nordbrand. *Risky Business: The Lundin Group's Involvment in the Tenke Fungurume Mining Project of the Democratic Republic of Congo*. Antwerp/

Stockholm: Diakonia, SwedWatch, and International Peace Information Service, 2008. Online: http://www.ipisresearch.be/download.php?id=201.

Derechos Humanos y Construcción de Paz: ¿Un Mismo Objetivo, Agendas Diferentes? Research Paper Series 4. Stockholm: Stockholm School of Theology, 2008. Online: http://www.ths.se/research/paper_no4.pdf.

Draft Review Study on Human Rights, Conflict and Peace-Building. OECD Synthesis Report, 2008.

Eide, Asbjørn. "Article 28." In *The Universal Declaration of Human Rights: A Common Standard of Achievement,* edited by Gudmundur Alfredsson and Asbjørn Eide. The Hague: Martinus Nijhoff, 1999.

Feher, Michael. "Terms of Reconciliation." In *Human Rights in Political Transition: Gettysburg to Bosnia,* edited by Carla Hesse and Robert Post. New York: Zone Books, 1999.

Field Report, July–September 2008. Ramallah, West Bank: Al-Haq Monitoring and Documentation Department, 2008. Online: http://www.alhaq.org/pdfs/Al_Haq_ Monitoring_and%20Documentation_Quarterly_Report_July_September_2008_ FINAL.pdf.

Gaer, Felice D. "Reflections on Human Rights Abuses." In *Human Rights Quarterly* 19.1 (1997) 1–8.

Galtung, Johan. *Peace by Peaceful Means: Peace and Conflict, Development and Civilization.* Oslo: International Peace Research Institute; London: SAGE, 1996.

Goonesekere, Savitri. *A Rights-Based Approach to Realizing Gender Equality.* Prepared in cooperation with the UN Division for the Advancement of Women. 2007. Online: http://www.un.org/womenwatch/daw/news/savitri.htm.

Guatemala: Memoria del Silencio. Guatemala: Comisión para el Esclarecimiento Historico, 1999; Guatemala: F & G Editores, 2005. Online: http://shr.aaas.org/guatemala/ ceh/report/english/toc.html.

Guidelines to Assist National Minority Participation in the Electoral Process. Warsaw: OSCE Office for Democratic Institutions and Human Rights, 2001.

Gunner, Göran, and Kjell-Åke Nordquist. *Mänskliga rättigheter och fredsbyggande— skilda agendor men samma mål?* Research Paper Series 1. Stockholm: Stockholm School of Theology, 2007. Online: http://www.ths.se/research/paper_no1.pdf.

Hannum, Hurst. "Human Rights in Conflict Resolution: The Role of the Office of the High Commissioner for Human Rights in UN Peacemaking and Peacebuilding." In *Human Rights Quarterly* 28.1 (2006) 1–85.

Hansén, Jesper, Lisa Hederström, Anita Klum, and Anna Massarsch. *I rätt riktning: Ett utbildningsmaterial för enskilda organisationer om rättighetsbaserat utvecklings- samarbete.* Stockholm: Fonden för mänskliga rättigheter, 2007; Sundbyberg: Diakonia, 2006.

Hochschild, Adam. *King Leopold's Ghost: A Story of Greed, Terror, and Heroism in Colonial Africa.* Boston: Houghton Mifflin, 1998.

Human Development Report 2007/2008: Fighting Climate Change: Human Solidarity in a Divided World. New York: UN Development Programme, 2007. Online: http://hdr .undp.org/en/media/HDR_20072008_EN_Complete.pdf.

Human Rights in Palestine and Other Occupied Arab Territories: Report of the United Nations Fact-Finding Mission on the Gaza Conflict. UN General Assembly. UN doc. A/HRC/12/48. September 25, 2009. Online: http://www2.ohchr.org/english/ bodies/hrcouncil/docs/12session/A-HRC-12-48.pdf.

In Larger Freedom: Towards Development, Security and Human Rights for All: Report of the Secretary-General of the United Nations for decision by the Heads of State and Government in September 2005. UN doc. A/59/2005. March 21, 2005. Online: http://daccess-dds-ny.un.org/doc/UNDOC/GEN/N05/270/78/PDF/N0527078. pdf?OpenElement. See also the homepage at http://www.un.org/largerfreedom/.

Indigenous and Tribal Peoples Convention. ILO convention 169. Geneva, June 27, 1989. Online: http://www.ilo.org/indigenous/Conventions/no169/lang--en/index.htm.

Indicators for Human Rights Based Approaches to Development in UNDP Programming: A Users' Guide. March 2006. New York: UN Development Programme, 2006. Online: http://www.undp.org/oslocentre/docs/HR_guides_HRBA_Indicators.pdf.

Jabarin, Shawan. *Peace and Human Rights: Palestine as a Case Study.* Presented at the international conference on "The Local Relevance of Human Rights," University Centre Saint-Ignatius Antwerp, Belgium, October 17, 2008. Online: http://www.alhaq.org/pdfs/Peace%20and%20Human%20Rights%20-%20Palestine%20as%20a%20Case%20Study.pdf.

¿Justicia Transicional sin Transición? Verdad, Justicia y Reparación para Colombia.. Bogotá: Centro de Estudios de Derecho, Justicia y Sociedad, 2006. Online: http://www.dejusticia.org/admin/file.php?table=documentos_publicacion&field=archivo&id=201.

The Lund Recommendations on the Effective Participation of National Minorities in Public Life & Explanatory Note. OSCE High Commissioner on National Minorities, September 1999. Online: http://www.osce.org/hcnm/30325.

Manual for Conflict Analysis. SIDA article Sida4334en. Stockholm: Swedish International Development Cooperation Agency, 2006.

Mathwig, Frank. *Entitling Human Beings: Human Rights and Human Dignity in a Theological-Ethical Perspective.* FSPC Position 6. Berne: Verlag Schweizerischer Evanelischer Kirchenbund SEK, 2008.

Mertus, Julie, and Jeffrey W. Helsing, editors. *Human Rights and Conflict: Exploring the Links between Rights, Law and Peacebuilding.* Washington, DC: United States Institute of Peace Press, 2006.

Nordquist, Kjell-Åke. *The Crossroads of Human Rights and Peace-Building—an Ongoing Debate.* Research Paper Series 2. Stockholm: Stockholm School of Theology, 2008. Online: http://www.ths.se/research/paper_no2.pdf.

———. *From "Just War" to Justified Intervention: A Theory of International Responsibility.* Uppsala: Uppsala University, Department of Theology, 1998.

Nunca Más: Informe de la Comisión Nacional sobre la Desaparición de Personas. 2 vols. 1a ed. CONADEP. Buenos Aires: Eudeba, 2006. Online: http://www.desaparecidos.org/arg/conadep/nuncamas/.

Orozco Abad, Iván. *Sobre los Llímites de la Conciencia Humanitaria: Dilemas de la Paz y la Justicia en América Latina.* Bogotá: Universidad de los Andes (Columbia)/ Editorial Temis, 2005.

"Proclamation of Tehran" (*Final Act of the International Conference on Human Rights*). UN doc. A/CONF.32/41. May 1, 1968. Online: http://untreaty.un.org/cod/avl/ha/fatchr/fatchr.html.

Report: The Second Interagency Workshop on Implementing a Human Rights–Based Approach in the Context of UN Reform. UN Development Group, 2003. Online: http://www.humanrights.se/upload/files/2/R%C3%A4ttighetsperspektivet/Common%20Understanding%20FN%202003.pdf.

The Responsibility to Protect: Report of the International Commission on Intervention and State Sovereignty. ICCISS, December 2001. Ottawa: International Development Research Centre, 2001. Online: http://www.iciss.ca/report-en.asp.

Rights-Based Approach to Development Programming: Training Manual. Manila: United Nations Philippines, 2002. Online: http://www.handicap-international.fr/bibliographie-handicap/3ApprocheDroit/OutilsFormation/RBAManual2.pdf.

Rokka, Jaana. *Att konfronteras med sitt våldsamma förflutna för en hållbar fred—Israel och Palestina.* Research Paper Series 3. Stockholm: Stockholm School of Theology, 2008. Online: http://www.ths.se/research/paper_no3.pdf.

Russett, Bruce M. *Grasping the Democratic Peace: Principles for a Post–Cold War World.* Princeton, NJ: Princeton University Press, 1993.

Russett, Bruce M., and John R. Oneal. *Triangulating Peace: Democracy, Interdependence, and International Organizations.* Norton Series in World Politics. New York: Norton, 2001.

Teitel, Ruti G. *Transitional Justice.* Oxford: Oxford University Press, 2000.

Theis, Joachim. *Rights-Based Monitoring and Evaluation: A Discussion Paper.* Save the Children, April 2003. Online: http://www.crin.org/docs/resources/publications/hrbap/RBA_monitoring_evaluation.pdf.

Thoms, Oskar N. T., and James Ron. "Do Human Rights Violations Cause Internal Conflict?" *Human Rights Quarterly* 29.3 (2007) 674–705.

Tutu, Desmond. *No Future without Forgiveness.* London: Rider, 1999.

Universal Declaration of Human Rights. UN General Assembly res. 217 A (III), December 10, 1948.

Valenzuela, Pedro. *Neutrality in Internal Armed Conflicts: Experiences at the Grassroots Level in Colombia.* Doctoral dissertation. Uppsala University, Department of Peace and Conflict Research, Report 87. Uppsala: Uppsala University, 2010.

Vienna Declaration and Programme of Action. UN doc. A/CONF.157/23. World Conference on Human Rights, Vienna, June 25, 1993. Online: http://www2.ohchr.org/english/law/vienna.htm.

Wiberg, Håkan. *Konflikteori och fredsforskning.* Stockholm: Almqvist & Wiksell, 1990.

www.ingramcontent.com/pod-product-compliance
Lightning Source LLC
Chambersburg PA
CBHW061737270326
41928CB00011B/2270